Written Off

The Journey Begins

The Approved in Christ Series

BOOK ONE

LISA N. PHILLIPS

Unless otherwise noted, all Scripture references in this book are taken from The Holy Bible, Amplified Bible, copyright © 2017. Lockman Foundation.

Printed in the United States of America

First Printing, 2025

DISCLAIMER

This memoir is a work of personal recollection and interpretation. It represents my experiences, memories, thoughts, and opinions as I remember them at various stages of my life. While I have made every effort to portray events truthfully, even enlisting the help of others who were present and also had knowledge of certain events, memory is inherently subjective, and details may have been reconstructed, such as some dialogue, for bringing out the essence of its content, clarity, natural flow, or to protect privacy.

Certain names and identifying details have been changed to respect privacy and to respect the anonymity of individuals. In those cases where I have used real names, those individuals gave me permission.

This memoir is not intended to harm, defame, embarrass, or misrepresent any person, group, or entity. The views expressed are my own, and great effort and angst has gone into protecting the individuals portrayed in this memoir. Any supposed or seeming inaccuracies are unintentional. They are not to be interpreted as untruths done deliberately.

This memoir contains some mental health information; however, I am not licensed in any medical field, and any discussions on such matters is based on personal experience, research, memories from others, and the information or knowledge that I had while growing up, and should not be taken as professional advice. This memoir spans several decades and mental health knowledge has evolved. Readers who seek guidance should consult a qualified mental health professional. Additionally, any discussions regarding mental health, do not necessarily reflect those of any other persons, organizations, or institutions.

By reading this book, you understand and acknowledge that it is a subjective account of personal experiences, and agree to interpret it as such. The author assumes no responsibility for how the content is interpreted, understood, or applied.

DEDICATION

To my husband, Ray:
During this book project, we've had sunshine and rain, and a few earthquakes have struck us unexpectantly, but through every joy, time of fear, and uncertainty, you have stood beside me, believing in me when weariness set in. That means everything to me. And this book is not just a reflection of my journey, but ours.

To my dad:
Words will never be enough to express how grateful I am to have your affirming words, warm hugs, and our tradition of long talks over the years. You have accepted me unconditionally and listened with patience. Thank you.

To my adult children, Megan and Lawrence:
"To know and to be known is relationship."
—Timothy Keller
Wholesome relationships come from the willingness to know and to *be known*. Through these pages, I hope you will know me and see with spiritual eyes the lengths God will go—using every experience, struggle, fear, and even darkness to lead a wounded soul to freedom. May you understand why I love you both so fiercely. You will always have a place to belong, arms that will hold you, and a love that will never let you go. Stay close, stay united, and stay in faith. Family is our greatest strength.

To my brother, Michael:

Life has taken us through unexpected storms, trials that tested us, and pain that once felt insurmountable. There were years of distance when the past felt heavier than the bond we shared. But even in what seemed lost, something greater was at work—healing, growth, and the unshakable truth that we were always meant to find our way back to each other. And we did.

Thank you for our heartfelt talks and for reclaiming lost childhood memories—I hold them close. No matter what life brings, one thing remains: we are brother and sister. We are family. And that will always be enough.

Love, Sis

To my half-brothers—You know who you are:

You both are fully in my heart, even though trauma, strife, sin, family disunity, and time have pained and worked against us. This book carries pieces of the good memories from when I was with you that I still cherish. It is my prayer that God's power will demolish all works of darkness that stand between you and Christ's freedom and that the spiritual truths within these pages will be a catalyst to removing the heaviness from your souls—and a light to personal healing, growth, and wholeness.

**To all who are walking through the pain
of rejection or ongoing estrangement:**

I dedicate these words in this book to you. Lean into Jesus; seek the hem of His robe as an act of faith for healing, allowing Him to grow you stronger as a result of your pain and loss. I know the soul ache you carry. I really do get it. Embrace God's truth, then trust He'll lead you to wholeness and peace. Then, allow Him to live powerfully through you as a result of your pain, giving others hope to seek their own wellness and peace and ultimately for God's glory.

TABLE OF CONTENTS

Acknowledgments

This memoir has lived quietly in my heart for decades, shaped by longing and loss, but also the persistent light of hope. From the very beginning there were people who listened to my heart without judgment and consoled me with heartfelt words of understanding and support.

I am especially grateful to Bob Harpole, of Best Seller Publishing, for extending me grace (and years) to get this book completed when life's storms and medical setbacks delayed this writing project on several occasions.

My sincere thanks to Rob Kosberg, for your innovative and empowering book publishing model. Your authentic and infectious desire to help authors get their message out into the world is inspiring. To you and the entire BSP team, thank you for walking alongside me in this publishing endeavor. I deeply appreciate the personalized assistance and support you and your team offered in each phase of book development.

To my beloved husband, Ray–thank you. Words fall short to convey how grateful I am for your support. These writing years were difficult and required a sacrifice of shared time together so that I could fulfill this purpose. Thank you for hanging in, for believing in the worthiness of this story, and in me.

Thanks to my friends, Theresa Wilson, Cindy Winger, and Linda Votaw. God weaved each of you into my life story with intention and grace. Thank you for being part of the earliest chapters of my life. As you read the pages of this book, I hope you'll see God's timing in placing each of you in my circumstances just when I needed a friend.

My sincere thanks to Jeannie Furst. You have always been my spiritual sister, speaking truth to my wounded heart. Thank you for your godly discernment over the years, shoulders to cry on, long talks on the phone, and helping me piece together details of events I had tucked away in pain. Thank you for gently filling in the blanks, and ministering to me through some very dark moments.

To my dear friend Kathy Opie - Our friendship began in the tender season of new motherhood, bonding over the quiet ache by mothers who couldn't be there as we needed. God formed this friendship for shared strength amidst our kind of ache and loss. Yet, our faith and God's grace taught us to hold our heads high and become the kind of mothers our own children could count on. Thank you for your prayers and support.

To Tami Rystrom–your fervent prayers and love for the Lord has been a gift to my soul. Over the years, you have listened to my story with interest and compassion, seeing my disappointed heart. Thank you for your spiritual insight, sometimes revealed in ways I hadn't recognized, where loss had clouded the edges of my understanding. Thank you for your godly influence that continues to this day.

To my copy editor, Barbara Bowen—thank you for your meticulous eye, steady patience, and your keen interest in my story. I'm grateful for your thoughtful guidance, your skill, and the way you helped bring clarity and strength to my voice. You also affirmed a difficult decision I made in the pages of this story-one that cost me dearly, and your feedback was affirming. Thank you for treating my story with the utmost care, for seeing its purpose, and helping me write it with grace and honesty.

Lord, my healing began with a whisper—thank You for the promise tucked into Isaiah 43:18–19. You spoke those words into my life when I needed them most, and they became a banner over my life ever since. This promise has reached far beyond the pages of this book; it has steadied me, encouraged me, and reminded me that You are always making a way—even when the way is unclear. I still cling to it today with the same confidence as when You first whispered it into my grandmother's spirit. You have never once let it fall empty.

REJECTION—
THE CRUELEST WORD

*Having prayed for believers of many nations, I have come
to this conclusion: the greatest undiagnosed, therefore,
untreated malady in the body of Christ today is rejection.
Rejection, whether active or passive, real or imaginary,
robs Jesus Christ of His rightful lordship in the life of His
children and robs them of the vitality and quality of
life that Jesus intended.*

—Noel and Phyl Gibson (Eckhardt 11)

In 1986, soon after my grandmother went to her heavenly home, I received one of her journals. I had read parts of it over the years, but as I prepared to write this book about my journey through parental rejection, I discovered an entry I hadn't seen before. It was a particularly difficult entry, written just before she went to bed one evening; however, she would not get a good night's rest. Memories, good and bad, kept coming to mind, stealing her sleep. The foremost angst on her heart was that of her estranged daughter—my mother. Mama had terminated their relationship. On the evening of December 27, 1982, she penned in her journal a phrase that has remained with me.

"Rejection—it has to be the saddest,
cruelest word in the dictionary."

My grandmother was right. Rejection is cruel. And if the rejection occurs as a child or teen, it causes a particular wounding to the body, soul, and spirit. Childhood rejection is more than just a painful experience—it's a powerful force that can disrupt the natural flow of emotional growth. Left unresolved, it can lay the foundation for a lifetime of inner turmoil, strained relationships, and ongoing mental and emotional struggles. The soul ache of estrangement, abandonment, or rejection can linger, stealing peace, robbing us of being in the moment, and either stunting or eroding our identity, even our zest for life. Simply put, rejection plunders our lives and ransacks our spirit. And it opens the door to serious mental health issues. If not addressed, rejection has the potential to throw a young person's life completely off course. I know this because I lived it and suffered quietly for many years.

Chances are, if you picked up this book, you're in a storm of rejection right now. And you may be in such hurt you don't believe you'll ever recover from the wounding or find inner peace. Maybe you are looking for what to do or how to move forward. Or perhaps you simply want your experience acknowledged. As it was true of me, it's quite possible that you don't even realize the full extent of the damage you've suffered. Like me, you've encountered one trauma after another, and after all your attempts to reconcile, you were met with scorn and judgment. And this has made you fearful, reticent to step into new things or new relationships, always seeking the approval of others as a temporary balm, or you carry around a spirit of condemnation, made to feel guilty and responsible for what wasn't yours to own.

Rejection is especially cruel because it's unnatural. As children, unconditional love and approval from our parents are essential—they form the foundation of emotional and character development, security, and identity. This design reflects God's purpose for the family, known as the parental blessing. When a parent steps back, revokes, or is unable to provide this vital blessing, the resulting wound creates an emotional vacuum. In this void, Satan can step into that life and plant the seed of a "spirit of rejection," fostering feelings of unworthiness and disconnection, among other effects.

Author John Eckhardt says in his book, *Destroying the Spirit of Rejection*, "An open door to rejection comes when we do not receive the love and acceptance God created us to receive" (Eckhardt 11). The effects of rejection extend beyond the emotional realm—they shape how a child views themselves, their potential, others, and even God. Without the reassurance of parental love, children may struggle with self-doubt, low self-esteem, low self-confidence, and carry a persistent ache for affirmation. In my case, my wounded soul and compliant nature took the road of fear. A fear of failure was my constant nemesis. But my struggle to feel accepted included manifestations of perfectionism, striving to be "that good daughter" to win approval. I fell into people-pleasing behavior, accepting the preferences of others because it was communicated to me that my own voice and preferences were unworthy or not realistic. Does this all sound familiar? We know this today as "gaslighting," a term non-existent in describing emotional abuse in the 1970's and 80's.

As I would discover, my mother also experienced rejection, but in a different form than how she rejected me. My maternal grandfather was also rejected, as was my maternal grandmother from her father. Left unhealed, the impact of rejection can echo through generations, as those who grow up without the parental blessing have a natural bent to pass it on to the next generation, creating what's called "familial rejection," a generational curse. Children who grow up without receiving the gift of unconditional love and acceptance, words of affirmation, hugs and embraces, even connecting with a parent emotionally or relationally may struggle to provide the same to their own families, continuing a legacy of emotional and spiritual emptiness unless the cycle is broken.

Worse still, parental rejection can distort a child's ability to trust and receive the love of God. The spiritual consequences of parental rejection can be profound, leading to a sense of spiritual alienation. Without the anchor of the parental blessing, individuals may struggle to understand the concept of God as a loving Father. Prayer may feel empty, and the promises of Scripture may seem out of reach. Some may even become vulnerable to counterfeit forms of comfort, seeking identity in worldly pursuits instead of resting in the truth of who God says they are.

At the heart of a child's relationship with their parents is a reflection of God's love. When that love is absent or withdrawn, it can distort how a child perceives their Heavenly Father. Instead of seeing God as loving, present, and trustworthy, they may view Him as distant, disapproving, or unpredictable. This warped perspective can create barriers to receiving God's grace and love, making it difficult for the wounded to trust His promises or believe they are fully accepted.

Rejection also opens the door to spiritual bondage. In fact, vulnerable children become prey to our enemy, Satan. Because children's minds and hearts are tender and have not matured, rejected children become Satan's target. First Peter 5:8 says, "Be sober [well balanced and self-disciplined], be alert and cautious at all times. That enemy of yours, the devil, prowls around like a roaring lion [fiercely hungry], seeking someone to devour." That someone could be you. Satan's goal is to ruin the lives of children, even adult children, and individuals made vulnerable by broken and/or fatherless homes, families in constant strife, dysfunction, sin, addiction, abuse, rejection, or abandonment. This is why God takes parenting and abuse seriously because rejection has a great potential to lead a young life away from Him.

Yet, there is hope—there is a path through the pain of rejection. God's love is more powerful than any wound. He woos the broken heart to receive His perfect love—a love that heals wounds and redefines identity, with a renewed sense of purpose. His love is mighty to break the grip of rejection, and the heart can be made well again. It's hard work, as I discovered, but worth the journey. The rejected find belonging, the abandoned find adoption, and the wounded find wholeness. And as He did for me, He'll even take away the gnawing soul ache of brokenness. His grace is sufficient to fill the void left by rejection (2 Corinthians 12:9).

My hope is that as you read my journey to wholeness, you'll take the first steps on your path to healing. Because you can't live an unhindered and worthy life until you give the Lord your estrangement or rejection. But once you do, He'll go to work and turn your life into a tapestry of marvelous colors, a blend of darks and lights, a combination of truth and pain, but also grace and beauty. And on the other side of rejection is seeing with spiritual eyes the marvelous ways He worked His healing. I want that for you, too. I also hope that you'll join me, in spirit, acknowledging Psalm 34:8, "taste and see that the lord [our God] is good …" (Psalm 34:8). And "by His wounds you have been healed" (1 Peter 2:24).

Lisa Phillips

CHAPTER ONE

Connecting the Dots

Hungry not only for bread—but hungry for love. Naked not only for clothing—but naked of human dignity and respect. Homeless not only for want of a home of bricks—but homeless because of rejection.

—Mother Teresa

"Before your dad arrives, I want my fruit trees watered," Mama insisted when she saw me stirring in bed.

"I'm up," I mumbled, rolling over in bed and propping myself up on one elbow. As my brain woke up, I took another moment to run through my mental calendar. It was Friday, July 4, 1980.

Remembering Dad was due to arrive for a weekend visit, my heart did a quick leap. I risked another second of inner glee as I imagined what my life would look like once I started college that fall. But in my early morning enthusiasm, I failed to appreciate Mama's stern tone.

Since 1978, we lived in the basement of our partially built house on 40 acres in McAllister, Kansas. My stepfather, Kevin, was constructing it in phases. After clearing the land in 1977 and pouring the foundation and walls the next summer, we moved out of an old trailer. Since this was another temporary situation, there were no interior walls or doors except for the single bathroom for all five of us. I considered these spaces more like sleeping quarters than bedrooms.

A lot had changed in two years. Before moving to McAllister, we were living in a quaint little house in the college town of Lawrence. It was a historical town that sprung up in the shadow of the University of Kansas. Both of my parents' families put down roots there nearly a century before. Rich in history, I found Lawrence delightful and charming.

We would not have been living in Lawrence if Mama hadn't suffered a mental health crisis in 1971. My parents were still married, and at that time, we lived in California. Two years before, in the summer of 1969, Daddy's request for a job transfer as a certified Airframe and Powerplant Mechanic with Trans World Airlines (TWA) was approved.

Our home in Gladstone, Missouri, the one we fondly referred to as the "green house," sold, and we moved west. Initially, Mama liked mountain living, but something eventually triggered a dark place within her. Her demeanor began to change. In reflective discussions with Dad when I was older, I wanted to know more about what happened when Mama became ill. Besides indicating she had become temperamental, she had also grown argumentative. Initially, Daddy thought she was homesick. It was summer, and school was out. He put Mama, Michael, my older brother, and me on a flight to Kansas to visit my maternal grandparents, hoping it would help her.

By the end of our visit, Mama seemed better, and we returned to California. But she continued to decline emotionally. Once school started in the fall of 1971, I often came home to find Mama napping, which was unusual for her. Although Mama's mental health struggles weren't discussed with Mike and me, we gathered something was changing, especially after witnessing my parents openly arguing, something I hadn't seen before. But that was just the beginning.

My family was unprepared for the approaching storm and its trail of calamity. At just thirty-two, Mama experienced a severe nervous breakdown. While Daddy operated out of desperation, striving to maintain stability in our home and get Mama the help she needed, my mother's emotional state continued to deteriorate. What ensued was an overwhelming and malevolent force that converged into a perfect storm, sucking my family into its mighty undertow.

Daddy flew Mama back to Kansas again; only this time she was admitted into the psychiatric hospital, the Menninger Foundation, located in Topeka. My maternal grandparents looked after her while Daddy remained behind to keep working to pay the medical bills. To help us back home, Aunt Lynnette and Uncle Robert, Mama's brother and his first wife, came to stay with us. My aunt got us off to school after Daddy left for work at the San Francisco International Airport and helped with meals and household chores. Sometime later, Mama returned home.

As a nine-year-old, Mama appeared well to me. I was happy to see her and relieved she was back home with us. We were a family again. Catching up one evening, I sat close to her. As we talked, she fanned her fingers gently through my long hair. I felt loved and secure. Just like when we lived in the green house in Gladstone. Mama was less anxious, and home life calmed down. And I didn't find her napping after returning from school. But that was probably because of the prescribed medication from her doctor.

We were all better—for a time, but the stress and chaos eventually returned. I learned later Mama had stopped seeing her psychiatrist and ceased taking her medication. No amount of pleading or encouragement from Daddy convinced her to stay on course with her treatment plan. She was adamant she didn't need medication. From then on, Daddy became angst-filled about many things, but mostly he worried about Mama being home alone during the day, especially after the kitchen fire. A hot skillet was forgotten on the kitchen stove, and the grease caught fire.

Seeing the smoke filling up the kitchen from my bedroom, I screamed for Daddy. He rushed in with Mama on his heels. As I stood off to the side, I watched Daddy scramble around the kitchen desperately searching for something—anything—to fight the fire.

But when the flames began to crawl up the window curtain, I became horrified. Daddy turned on the kitchen faucet, tossed several dish towels he had found in a drawer into the sink, then frantically slapped the curtains with the wet towels. Thankfully, he managed to put the fire out before it reached the ceiling. Our home, sitting in the dry Santa Cruz Mountains, was spared, but the kitchen was a mess. And Daddy became more worried and troubled.

After the fire, my parent's marriage grew more tension-filled. The stress finally took a toll.

In the early morning hours, while driving the curvy mountain highway heading for work, Daddy was preoccupied with Mama's mental health. Even though he knew his commute well, he failed to slow down on the approach of a sharp curve. His 1970 GTO nearly plunged over the mountainside. Thankfully, the guardrail was enough to stop his car, instantly flipping it upside down. Banged up, Daddy crawled out from under the car and the shattered windshield that had fallen on top of him. Minutes later, a passerby arrived and immediately called an ambulance from a nearby roadside emergency phone. Miraculously, he suffered no internal injuries, except for bruises and an extremely sore body, but he would be okay. His car, however, the only one he had ever bought new, was destroyed.

The car accident was the last straw. Daddy abruptly put our home up for sale. Mike and I were pulled out of school, and we moved to the sprawling city of Menlo Park, hoping city life would better suit Mama. After moving into another new home, Michael and I entered new schools again. And for a time, the move was good. We were making new friends. Daddy even took a sailing course, and upon completing the training, bought his first sailboat. One Saturday, he took us sailing on Lake Berryessa in Napa County. But once we were in the water, the wind kicked up and the waves became rough. At nine-years old, I had mixed feelings about the experience, especially when the port side heeled deeply, putting the boat at water level. I feared falling into the open water. But when I glanced back at Daddy, he gave me a tender smile. Instead of panicking, I decided to trust that smile. To me, it meant he was in control and I was still safe. But like the rough waters of Lake Berryessa, the calm we had was overcome by the fierce winds of adversity. Mama couldn't cope there either. Within months, our family imploded.

Our departure from California was unexpected and chaotic. One August day in 1972, Mike and I left another school, and boarded a flight, with Daddy in distress trying to keep Mama from taking off with his children. Mike, being older, was suspicious of our hasty departure, but not me. I didn't grasp what was really happening. The best thing I figured was that we were simply returning for another visit with my grandparents. The only part that didn't make sense was seeing Michael in tears as we looked for our seats on the plane. Deep down he knew what was taking place. We were leaving for good. Unbeknownst to me, we would not return to California, but more importantly, that day we boarded the plane was our last as a family.

My maternal grandparents met us at the Kansas City International Airport and gladly made room for the three of us in their modest home on Savanna Street. It was a crowded situation, but we made do. A couple of weeks after our arrival, Mama announced that she had enrolled us in new schools for the upcoming '72–'73 school season. Another abrupt decision troubled Mike.

"Why are we going to school here?" he asked.

Mama gave Mike a vague reply, something about not wanting us to miss too much school while we were in Kansas.

This new development may have confirmed Mike's suspicions of a divorce, but not mine. I didn't know what divorce was. I had never heard of the word. Shortly thereafter, boxes began arriving. Then one day a large box came addressed to me. Inside was my bicycle. I was thrilled but thought it odd Daddy had sent it. As the weeks passed, I began to suspect something was off. But I didn't know what, and I didn't know how to ask. And nobody was talking. I limped along in a muddled mindset.

In September, I turned eleven years old. It was my first birthday without Daddy. I began to sense this trip to my grandparents wasn't like our visit the year before when Daddy thought Mama was homesick. Still, I believed we were returning to California or Daddy would be joining us, even though his letters didn't indicate such. When I got older, I learned why. It wasn't possible for him to move back, not because he didn't want to be with his children but that he couldn't. His employer, TWA, wouldn't approve another job transfer back to Kansas.

One day while eating breakfast, I overheard Mama and Grandpa discussing several cars she had looked at for sale. Grandpa then asked her which one she wanted to buy. That's the moment I began to connect the dots. I realized *why* Daddy sent my bike and *why* Mama needed a car. We were in Kansas to stay.

I began to connect other dots, too—Daddy would not be returning to Kansas. This reality was a punch in the gut and set me back emotionally. Even though my father hadn't resigned that the marriage was over, Mama had. Just three months into our stay at my grandparents' home, she began dating.

Christmas of 1972 didn't feel right without Dad. It bothered me that he was alone, especially during the holidays, and the longer we were apart as a family, the sadder I became. My parents' divorce commenced. In the spring of '73, Mama remarried, possibly disregarding the mandatory six-month waiting period California required.

My brother, Mike, and I experienced our parents' divorce when family culture was different. Less aware of societal issues, the political climate, or cultural shifts, our world was much smaller. Besides school, we learned much about the world from our parents. Families today are more transparent about issues. In the 60's and 70's open family discussions largely didn't exist. Parents had tighter control over family matters. Children were less privy to grown-up issues like marital or job troubles, financial stresses, separation, and divorce. And I doubt the mental illness of a parent was high on the list of family discussions either.

Quietly and in our own way, Mike and I began to process our new reality, but neither of us spoke to the other about the heartache over the demise of our family or what we left behind in California. Sadly, in the early 70's, counseling for children of divorce wasn't mainstream either, and I have no recollection of meeting with a school counselor. We were expected to accept and adapt to a new life in a new place with a new stepfather.

Unfortunately, parenting plans also didn't exist yet. Visitation was done through the honor system. Dad trusted Mama to put us on a plane to California. This was because child custody battles were rare in the 1970's. The courts followed what was called the "Tender Years Doctrine," in which mothers were automatically granted full custody of their children unless it was found the mother was unfit. It appears the courts focused more on the fate of property and assets than on fair custody agreements, parenting plans, or the rights of good fathers. Even more odd was how the court seemed to overlook concerns regarding Mama's mental health. And back then, it didn't appear any laws were in place or enforced restricting a parent from taking children across state lines, as happened in our case, leaving a loving, stable father voiceless and disenfranchised.

As for children of divorce, the thinking back then tended to be that sparing children pain was being a responsible adult. My parents may have subscribed to this belief, innocently enough, convinced it would be less painful than getting the whole ugly truth at once. There was also the adage, "They're children; they'll adapt." Today, we know this is not a healthy way to handle divorce when children are involved. Parents who take off with their kids to another state without permission can bring criminal charges and/or lose custody.

That first year, Mike and I went through emotional changes. My chatty disposition diminished, and the nickname "Motormouth" Mike fondly teased me with was also gone. Instead, a melancholy mood blanketed my spirit. I withdrew and became shy. Mike changed too. He had never been the talker like I was, but he became more private, especially with his thoughts. The sibling fun we shared cooled.

If it had not been for the family that lived across the street from my grandparent's, my transition would have been more difficult.

Theresa and I first met in 1966. We were both around five years old. Short like me, she came from a large family of seven. Before we moved to California in 1969, while living in the green house in Gladstone, Missouri, we would often drive to Lawrence to visit my grandparents. While there, Grandma sent me over to Theresa's home to play. From 1966 to 1969, with each visit, Theresa and I picked up on our friendship where we left off. Then, in 1969, our intermittent friendship paused when Daddy's job transfer to California was approved. While the world watched the news coverage of Apollo 11 in July of '69, our home in Gladstone, Missouri, sold, and we left as a family, driving west to a new world of our own in California. Looking back, the life we left behind in the Midwest would turn out to be my family's final season of being a cohesive, happy, and secure family.

Three years later, in 1972, upon moving in with my grandparents, Grandma sensed I could use a friend and, like before, sent me across the street to Theresa's home. To welcome me back, Theresa put on a modest party of cookies and punch. This time, I met her friend, Cindy.

Cindy also lived on Savanna Street. Next came Denise. An old-fashioned friendship quickly formed between the four of us. Even though I was confused about enrolling in a new school, having friends quelled the new-school jitters; however, Mike was not so fortunate. He had to make all new friends. That fall I walked to and from school in the security of my Savanna Street friends.

Always positive, Theresa's caring and sensitive character fostered a natural ability to highlight the bright side of difficult situations. Cindy was a year younger and, like me, was experiencing changes in her own family. Like a big sister, Theresa took her under her wings. Privately, I was trying to untie the knots of sadness and confusion. I was in a season of constant change, and with each abrupt transition, there had been no closure from the previous one. Reflecting on this ready-made group of girlfriends, there was a therapeutic quality about it; they made me laugh, releasing some of the heartache of how my family used to be.

In early 1973, just before Mama married Kevin, he purchased a home on Hickory Lane. Five months had passed since we left California, and although I knew what a wedding was, I hadn't factored in a new stepfather. Just after their nuptials, I left Highland Elementary School and the Savanna Street girls in the same quick fashion as leaving California. However, I appreciated the new house because I was ready to have my own bedroom again, but leaving my friends on Savanna Street was another disappointing loss I hadn't been prepared for.

It was distressing starting over. I didn't know a soul at the new school. It was March. How would I make friends before school was out for the summer? The progress I had made stalled. I was sad my parents weren't together, sad that Daddy wasn't with us, sad at leaving the Savanna Street girls, and anxious and fearful about another school. Again, Grandma sensed my anxiety.

One day, she stopped by our new home. Happy to see my grandmother, I ran outside to greet her. She stepped out of her car, bent over to face me, and with a tender smile and gentle voice, said, "I have something special for you." I rolled up and down on the balls of my feet, anxious to see what Grandma brought. She opened the back driver's side passenger door and reached into a small box. After shutting the door, I looked down to the driveway. There sat the most adorable orange and white tabby kitten. Immediately, I burst into squeals of delight. I reached down and swooped up the delicate kitten and cuddled it in the crook of my neck.

"I thought this might help you feel better," Grandma said, with a satisfied grin.

"Thank you, Grandma! He's so cute."

"Will you love him and take care of him?"

"Yes! I will. I promise!"

"Now you have to pick out a name."

After some thought, I named my new pet Jody. Every day after school, Jody greeted me in the driveway and followed me inside. While I did homework, he curled up in my lap. He was an affectionate and playful kitty, but he did have one quirky, ornery side.

During the summers, Jody hid in the bushes below my bedroom window. Crouching low, he remained still, waiting for an unsuspecting person to walk by.

One day, as Mama passed in front of those bushes carrying a basket of freshly laundered clothes to hang on the clothesline, Jody sprung from the bushes, startling Mama. She dropped the basket of wet laundry as Jody's paws looped around one ankle, his razor-sharp claws piercing her skin. Hearing blood curdling screams, I scrambled from my room and rushed outside to find Mama frozen, glaring at me with Jody sprawled at her feet. With any slight move, Jody sunk his claws deeper into her ankles. I carefully plucked his claws off. Now in a vinegary mood, Mama picked up the wet clothes from the yard and sauntered off to the clothesline. I carried Jody back into the house, snickering softly to myself. Mama always said she hated Jody, but I never took her seriously—not until seven years later, when she finally got even with Jody and broke my heart.

My new fifth-grade teacher at Cedar Wood Elementary, Mrs. Kohler, placed me at a desk beside a girl named Linda. Looking around at my new classmates, I missed my Savanna Street friends. Plus, I was fearful of recess and finding myself alone on the playground. In need of a friend, I turned to Linda. From that insecure place, I found my first words to say hello.

Contrary to me and my long brownish-red and wavy hair, freckled face, and fair skin, Linda radiated a healthy glow with her naturally tanned complexion, long, straight dark hair, and brown eyes. When we broke for lunch, she invited me to eat with her. Afterwards, during recess, we played Four-Square with other girls on the playground. That day walking home, I was elated and relieved I'd made a new friend. Less anxious the next day, Linda and I ate lunch together again, and every day thereafter, until the end of the school year.

Like the Savanna Street girls, the friendship between Linda and me became easy and comfortable. But my melancholy disposition didn't suddenly disappear; it lingered during the 1973 winter holiday season, my second Christmas without Daddy, and halfway through my sixth-grade year. Years later, I realized the melancholy mood I was mired in was really childhood depression.

Because airline employees rarely got time off around the holidays, my visits with Daddy were at other times of the year. Mike and I flew to California for visits in the summers; then, as teenagers, we traveled abroad, where we were exposed to other cultures. This was important to Dad because much of his childhood was spent living in the jungles of South America with his mining engineer father and his mother, who homeschooled him.

Eventually, I adjusted to my new reality, but I still missed Dad. And I assumed the same for Michael. Then, around ninth grade, I noticed changes in Mama's moods. It started with the washing machine. She browbeat me over forgetting to turn the washing machine water temperature to the warm setting. From there, her personality turned unusually impatient, more agitated, and critical of me. Before long, having friends over made me uneasy; I preferred going to their homes, where I felt less guarded.

In 1976, another new change took place. My half-brother, Davey, was born. And unbeknownst to the rest of us, Mike was planning changes of his own.

In the spring of 1977, in the early morning hours of his eighteenth birthday, he carried his duffle bag to the front door. The day before, he had dropped out of his senior year of high school, telling no one. As mothers do, Mama suspected something. Before Michael could get out the door undetected, Mama suddenly appeared. With her arms outstretched on either side and her legs hip-width apart, forming a large X with her body, she blocked his exit. From that stance, she quietly grilled Mike with a set of questions about his plans. Satisfied with his answers, Mama dropped her arms and stepped aside. Michael picked up his bag, said goodbye, and slipped out the door. On the other side of the wall, I slept, oblivious to it all.

Meanwhile, life at home carried on, and Mama, to my recollection, said nothing about Michael's departure. Her secrecy and silence fueled feelings of insecurity in me and planted questions in my mind. My brother's sudden departure troubled me, especially since I didn't get to say goodbye. Now a part of me felt left behind. I wondered where he was or when I'd see him again. At dinner, I missed his presence at the table. In passing his room, I'd stop at his door, looking for any sign he was back. Why couldn't Mama just tell me he left and where he went? But I sensed tension in the home around Mike's leaving, and I feared asking questions. Mama was touchy. Asking questions triggered her to snap at me. I missed Mike at school, too. I was a sophomore, and we were finally attending high school together. In between classes, I looked for him in the crowded halls. Spotting each other, we'd exchange smiles and waves. Now that was gone.

Internally, Michael was struggling. Since our parents' divorce five years earlier, he needed Dad's guidance. He was on a personal quest to sort out his life—to find his way—yet dropping out of high school seemed like a step backwards to me.

Dad learned of Michael dropping out of school, not through Mama, as she never shared that kind of news with Dad, I believe, for spite to keep him at a disadvantage. I also think this is why Mama didn't tell me about his leaving—so I wouldn't alert Dad, a later realization that felt mean. I'd like to believe our grandfather stepped in and informed Dad. Grandpa invested in Mike, establishing a bond in the same way Grandma had done with me. Immediately Dad flew back, found Mike, along with a few shady squatters, living in the empty home of our paternal grandmother, Helen. Falling ill, she had moved to Pennsylvania to live with her daughter, my aunt, Doris. Dad was still in the throes of getting her house ready to sell. He kicked the squatters out, closed the house up once again, and the two of them flew back to California, where Michael eventually earned his high school GED. Now living with Dad, a part of me wished I was there, too. Not long later, Mike enlisted in the Army. I was happy for him, but I knew it would be a long time before I'd see him again.

Now the oldest child at home, my stepfather and I had an unspoken understanding. We arrived at this amicable relationship while working together on various home improvement projects. I respected my stepdad, and he recognized I already had a father and didn't come off trying to take his place. He never criticized my dad in my presence, nor did he raise his voice at me. He was a kind, respectable man. But at twenty-nine years old, he had no idea, none of us did, of the same darkness descending once again upon our home.

It was during my junior high school years that I began attending church. I loved learning, and, right from the start, I took to Sunday school. My friends, Theresa and Cindy, later attended with me. Soon, the three of us were going on weekend camping retreats and Bible camp in the summers. Then, around the age of thirteen, I accepted Jesus while at a weekend church retreat, a decision that would later prove crucial.

A year after Mike left for California, my second half-brother, Timothy, was born, triggering a sudden announcement. We were moving again—this time to the small farming community of McAllister. Like before, there had been no discussion. The news horrified me. I was going into my junior year of high school. The timing couldn't have been worse.

*   *   *   *   *   *

Now living amongst crops and cows, I hadn't forgotten how Mama didn't do well in remote areas. How would she cope with nothing but pasture lands and distant neighbors? Then too, were the harsh winters and road closures due to excessive snow, shutting us off from the outside world. But like all previous moves, I accepted the situation in quiet compliance. In Mama's home there was no room for negotiation, and complaining was out of the question.

I started my junior year of high school with misgivings, and I wasn't able to secure friends in my own grade. Instead, I befriended several girls from the sophomore class. Yet, I never fully bonded to that high school. Fortunately, I became the recipient of the car that had belonged to Helen, my paternal grandmother, who had since passed away. It was a timely gift from Dad. The '67 Chrysler, a tank of a car, became my lifeline. I didn't care how unhip it was; it kept me connected to my friends in Lawrence.

After our move to the country, frequent arguments began to erupt between Mama and Grandma. I had never seen this before; I had always thought they had had a good relationship, especially since my grandparents had taken us in during my parents' divorce. What could be wrong between them? From the tone of Mama's voice and her scornful choice of words, I quickly gathered Mama's anger stemmed from deeper and more serious issues. This tension quickly spilled into Mama and Kevin's marriage and eventually to me. Mama didn't hide her anger with her mother, but she didn't explain her reasons. But I sensed a certain hostility I hadn't seen before. I was close with Grandma, but I quickly felt trapped and targeted in the conflict. While Mama ranted about her mother, I picked up on an expectation to concur, to stand in agreement with her. Additionally, my stepdad's family had taken an immediate dislike to Mama. As a new step-grandchild in Kevin's extended family, I was welcomed but never assimilated, thus I empathized with Mama's predicament. She demanded Kevin confront his family about this, but he was reluctant. The thing that infuriated Mama the most was non-compliance. This went on for some time, and, eventually, only Kevin attended his family gatherings.

The conflict between Mama and Grandma escalated. Her temperament skipped the simmer setting and went right into a boiling, seething hostility that was frightening. Grandma urged Mama to be calm and reasonable, but she wanted nothing to do with that. My mother's livid anger became all-consuming, sucking the oxygen out of our home. Hers was a loathing that demanded to be acknowledged. But what was most disturbing was Mama's outright unsympathetic demeanor. To me, she didn't seem to care who she hurt with her words.

This downturn in Mama's character and the blatant unwillingness to maintain self-control was alarming and set me on edge. She did not exhibit any restraint for the threats she made or apologize for the ugly, cruel words she spoke. I was perplexed about what was taking place, but some of what I saw and heard echoed my dad's description of his experiences with Mama when she had the nervous breakdown. But why was she so angry with Grandma? I knew there was more going on, but I wanted to stay out of it. Plus, the atmosphere was becoming antagonistic, and I knew Mama didn't like being questioned.

Not realizing it at the time, I had become the scapegoat for Mama's negative emotions. Such terms as "scapegoat" and "gaslighting" weren't common words then. Falling short of Mama's expectations or making an honest mistake triggered her scorn with personal attacks on my character and an occasional slap across the face, especially if I inconvenienced her, like the time I had forgotten my housekey when I got home from school. She was still in town doing errands. And my stepfather was at work. It was winter, and I had gone to the neighbors to wait for her, but I hadn't noticed she had already returned home, and finding me not there, went out looking for me in her car. When I saw her headlights in the darkness, I thanked the neighbors for allowing me to stay, then hurried home, expecting trouble. Angry as a hornet because I had put her to extra trouble, I received a harsh slap. A bloody nose ensued. I vowed to never forget my key again.

Each morning, I awoke with dread, fearing the mistakes I'd make that day and her frightening temper. Internally, I felt inadequate about myself and my place in our home. Mama didn't restrict my freedom to visit friends or go on church camps, but around the home, I fought a private battle. The only way to cope was to strive for her approval. But what hurt was her ability to use my weaknesses and vulnerabilities against me. After making a mistake, she shouted at me, saying I had some kind of devious motive. And if I attempted to explain, she accused me of lying. I didn't know what to do and often had no answer for her, which seemed to enrage her even more, and since Kevin didn't intervene on my behalf, I never went to him. In that regard, I had to think like Mama, something no minor should have to do. Going to my stepfather or even my grandmother would be viewed as deception.

In high school, I transitioned to "Campus Life." It was a large and active group of Christian high school students. This group had a profound effect on me. The relationships I built in Campus Life reinforced my young faith. Grandma took an interest in my church involvement and retreats, leading to faith conversations between us. With things escalating at home, Campus Life also became a place of refuge—an emotional break from the constant internal angst about how to cope with Mama. Because of her unpredictable moods, I didn't always know what would trigger her to flip emotionally. When she spoke disparaging words over me, they conveyed disapproval and plunged me into a world of "nots." I was not assertive, bold, or confident. And I was not articulate with words like Mama was. I placed other "nots" on myself. With a face full of freckles, I was not particularly pretty. I was not even average height. In fact, I was obsessed with my short stature, comparing myself to other girls. But for a few hours each week, church and Campus Life cultivated hope and trust in a God who cared for me and my circumstances. I clung to that truth as a lifeline for strength. I left those meetings encouraged to press on and hopeful that things between Mama and me would somehow improve. I continued to do my best for her, thinking she'd be proud of me. But every night, beneath the covers, I prayed, asking God to help me bear up under a difficult mother. She had become a Goliath to me. Yet, as I prayed, she didn't change, nor did my circumstances. But, in hindsight, God had heard my prayers, and He did have a plan that would change my life, but the appointed time hadn't come yet. In my own private war, I kept doing what I thought was right—what my faith was teaching me about how to persevere and how to remain respectful towards my mother, even though I was in enormous inner distress. She wasn't always deserving of my respect, but in 1979, disrespect would have earned me another slap and my car taken away. Regrettably, I should have done what Michael did— put myself on a flight to California, using my airline identification card, that came with free tickets. However, I was too scared to take that step. I feared what Mama might do to those I loved.

Meanwhile, my stepfather continued to build up his small farm. I was thankful that my bedroom space was in the far corner of the basement. Without walls or doors, at bedtime I could hear Mama and Kevin talking quietly in bed, as well as the happy chatter of my young half-brothers.

CHAPTER TWO

THE PARENTAL BLESSING

It's a blessed thing to love and feel loved in return.

—E.A. Bucchianeri

We know it today as the Parental Blessing. And it's a powerful force—for good or for detriment, depending on whether it's given or withheld. Even long after they have left home, adult children who missed or were denied their parents' blessing may become overachievers in an attempt to feel validated, or they may bury themselves in their careers or other pursuits or even substance abuse in order to cope. And it's not unusual to know something is wrong but be unable to put a name to it.

The emotional hurt caused by parents who reject their children and deny them acceptance and love creates a profound sense of loss. Their souls know that what is missing is significant. And sadly, a parent's withheld blessing can even affect one's faith, keeping them from believing they are acceptable and loved in God's eyes. In my case, parental rejection became the catalyst to lean into my faith. I didn't know it then, but I had what is called a heart "bent" towards the Lord. I used my faith to search for meaning, direction, and eventually healing. Additionally, my mother's inability to accept me reinforced my desire for a close and connected family of my own someday. Knowing I'd still make mistakes, as parents are not perfect, I vowed that my children would always have the gift of unconditional love and approval. Yet, those who rarely witnessed loving and accepting bonds in their childhood may find it a struggle to create their own close bonds with their spouse and children. Showing physical affection and hearing such words as "I love you" or "I'm proud of you" may have been rare or didn't happen at all.

Reasons for Rejection

The reasons for missing the parental blessing are varied and complex and can span across generations. Below are some examples:

- Abandonment by one or both parents
- Abuse
- Parents who constantly criticize children convey that they can never measure up
- Opting to belong to a different religion than the one raised with
- Gay and lesbian children
- Mental illness
- Substance abuse
- Crossing into a higher socioeconomic class
- Marrying below one's socioeconomic class
- Interracial marriage
- Parents who fail to bond with their children
- Parents who are wrapped up in their own lives with work, hobbies, and pleasures
- Generational family expectations
- Birth of a child outside of marriage
- Not being a certain body type

Mothers whose lives turned out less than satisfactory or were filled with disappointment may become indifferent or resentful towards their daughters. Mothers who constantly nitpick or criticize their daughters send the message that they'll never measure up. And ongoing cruel digs can cause daughters to distrust their own decision-making ability. And it's not uncommon for daughters to find themselves as doormats to overbearing or dominant mothers. Authoritarian parents who resort to scorn crush their children's sense of autonomy and worthiness. These children are then unable to ask for what they need. As a teen, I didn't feel safe asking for what I needed emotionally from Mama, due in part to ongoing distrust with my fragile emotions. I didn't expect I'd receive a loving response. And sadly, some mothers even resort to stalking, harassing, and interfering in their daughter's life, marriage, and even in her faith, as my own mother later did.

For boys, rejection can result from the son choosing a different career than what his father expected or choosing a career or trade that one or both parents believe is beneath him. This can happen with long-standing generational family expectations. Rejection can also manifest because a father is rarely home or always away with his job. Distance causes limited opportunities between parents and children for growth, understanding, and acceptance. This is especially true for children of divorce. Loving and accepting fathers who are highly involved with their children produce children with higher levels of sociability, confidence, and self-control ("Father's Impact"). But when sons don't live up to a father's expectations, they may internalize this as a reflection on themselves.

Even if we haven't had contact with our parents for a while, the struggle remains fresh; it may still affect our lives today. This is because insecurity, fear, unworthiness, indecision, guilt, trust issues, and other symptoms of rejection cloud our hearts, and various fears hold us back. These and other emotions are associated with a spirit of rejection, which means we are still in bondage to those emotions. Loving acceptance from our parents is a basic right. Parents who

refuse to love also insult God and His design for parents. As children, when we are
unable to measure up, it has the potential
to color how we perceive what others are
thinking about us, as well as how we internalize what we believe about ourselves.
Others may say we are capable and qualified, but they don't know what hidden
perceived beliefs are inside; often young
adult children who have been rejected
have self-esteem issues and lack confidence. They doubt themselves and fear

> As children, when
> we're unable to
> measure up, it
> has the potential
> to color how we
> perceive what
> others are thinking
> about us, as well as
> how we internalize
> what we believe
> about ourselves.

they will fail or miss the professional mark. And many give up on
their dreams. In a later chapter, you'll read how the spirit of rejection
derailed a dream of mine.

Additionally, if months or years of rejection or estrangement
pass by with no resolution or change, the whole situation languishes
and festers within us. The heart remains split. Stuck in neutral, the
adult child doesn't know how to go forward. Fear of continued rejection holds her back. Then there are some who, like me, for many
years kept their hearts open and continued pouring themselves out
to the rejecting parent(s), in part due to the wrong understanding of
what it means to honor parents but also because they couldn't fathom being permanently forsaken. Yearning to hear those vital words
of loving acceptance and approval that feed our souls and give life
to our spirit, many still linger long into adulthood trying to get the
elusive parental blessing. Mama insisted my beliefs were wrong, my
reality was wrong, my emotions, viewpoints, and choices were all
wrong. She had stepped back from my life. Yet from a place of a deep
need to bond emotionally and relationally, I remained committed to
the dream of a loving mother-daughter relationship.

The parental blessing is the road map to raising emotionally
strong and confident children. It isn't a 21st century twist on how to
raise happy, well-adjusted kids but is actually centuries old.

Esau's Story

Esau's father, Isaac, was nearing death, and one day he called Esau to his side.

Isaac said, "See here, I am old; I do not know when I may die. So now, please take your [hunting] gear, your quiver [of arrows], and your bow, and go out into the open country and hunt game for me; and make me a savory and delicious dish [of meat], the kind I love, and bring it to me to eat, so that my soul may bless you [as my firstborn son] before I die."

(Genesis 27:2-4)

In Esau's day, the blessing was reserved for the firstborn son, and it included two parts. The first part was the receiving of the father's wealth and possessions, and the second part was a statement of acceptance and approval, a verbal declaration from the father to his firstborn son. Most of us know what happened to the first part of Isaac's blessing. Esau gave it away to his younger brother, Jacob, for a bowl of stew.

Esau was a skilled hunter (Genesis 27:3). As an outdoorsman, he may have also been a bit extroverted. Jacob, on the other hand, may have had a domestic side and preferred the kitchen, as hinted in Genesis 25:29. Perhaps this is why his mother, Rebekah, favored him. And Jacob, understanding Esau's impulsiveness, played his older brother right out of his birthright. After a day of hunting, Esau returned home very hungry. Rather than waiting for mealtime, he let his impatient side get the best of him and exchanged his birthright for a bowl of Jacob's freshly made stew. It went downhill from there.

Isaac pulled his eldest son, Esau, to his side one day and told him that it was time to finally pass on his blessing (Genesis 27). His father asked him to bring home wild game to prepare a celebratory meal, but what Isaac didn't know was that Rebekah had overheard her husband's request, and once Esau left, she instigated her own plan. She told her favored son, Jacob, to do the same, only Jacob simply went to their flock and selected two suitable young goats. Jacob even put on Esau's clothes and the skins of the goats over his hands to convince Isaac that he was Esau, for Esau was on the hairy side. The plan worked, due in part to Isaac's poor eyesight, but what about Jacob's voice? It wasn't anything like his brother's, but Isaac reconciled that the body with the goat skins must be Esau and went ahead and gave his personal blessing to Jacob. Isaac had been duped.

What a shock it must have been for Esau to come home from his hunt and discover that not only had his brother deceived him but his mother, too! "Then Isaac trembled violently, and he said, 'Then who was the one [who was just here] who hunted game and brought it to me? I ate all of it before you came, and I blessed him. Yes, and he [in fact] shall be (shall remain) blessed'" (Genesis 27:33).

Since Esau had given away his birthright—the wealth and possessions of his father—to Jacob for a bowl of soup, all that was left was his father's personal blessing. "Esau said to his father, 'Have you only one blessing, my father? Bless me, even me also, O my father.' Then Esau [no longer able to restrain himself] raised his voice and wept [loudly]" (Genesis 27:38).

Isaac, realizing what he had done, said to his favorite son, "I have made Jacob your lord and master; I have given him all his brothers and relatives as servants; and I have sustained him with grain and new wine. What then can I do for you, my son?" (Genesis 27:37).

Can you sense the betrayal and the depth of Esau's hurt? He's just been given a devastating blow. But he turned his hurt into anger and vowed to kill his brother for deceitfully stealing his father's blessing, a monumental rite of passage as important as a modern-day high school or college graduation in which we expect our parents to give us words of approval and love. Isaac then tries to console his son with a special word, but at first, it comes across like a curse.

Your dwelling shall be away from the fertility of the earth and away from the dew of heaven above; But you shall live by your sword, And serve your brother; However it shall come to pass when you break loose [from your anger and hatred], That you will tear his yoke off your neck [and you will be free of him].

(GENESIS 27:39-40)

Did you notice the words "away?" Isaac is sending Esau away. He's told to leave home. It rings of rejection, but one day, Esau will be delivered of his yoke of hatred towards his brother. The passage above portrays a personal, heartfelt message to Esau that, although his father can't reverse the blessing, he affirms Esau that he will overcome this rejection.

> **When we value someone, our desire is to add to their life. Likewise, when we step back from someone, we subtract from their life. – John Trent and Gary Smalley, *The Blessing – Giving the Gift of Unconditional Love and Acceptance.***

The Meaning of "to Bless"

Interestingly, most of us have never really considered what blessing our children looks like, other than with words of encouragement, giving our children nice things, opportunities, heartfelt discussions, and spending time with them. True, these things are certainly part of it, but when the word to bless is broken down into its biblical meaning, it is so much richer.

To "bless" someone is to show them that they are important to you. They have value. And because you value them, you will honor them by treating them accordingly. One of the meanings of "to bless" which is a great word picture, carries the idea of adding weight or coins to a scale to bestow value to someone. When we value someone, our desire is to add to their life. Likewise, when we step back

from someone, we subtract from their life. It also means to step forward with acceptance, approval, and unconditional love (Trent and
Smalley 37–38).

Stepping Towards or Stepping Back

Because we're born with the natural need to be loved, approved of,
and accepted, when we are denied this basic right as children, it opens
up the door for the enemy, Satan, to gain entry into our heart. He'll
take advantage of a child's vulnerabilities and sow seeds of a spirit
of rejection, such as hatred, anger, bitterness, and resentment into
that life. This is what initially happened to Esau. Essentially, when
parents step back, Satan will step forward. And if deliverance doesn't
happen, the seed is replanted into their children, and if it becomes a
lifestyle, it becomes an iniquity.

> The word *iniquity*
> means to bend
> or to distort (the
> heart). – Marilyn
> Hickey, *Breaking
> Generational curses.*

In her book *Breaking Generational
Curses*, Marilyn Hickey states, "the word
iniquity means to bend or to distort (the
heart). It also implies a certain weakness
or predisposition toward a certain sin"
(21). When a sin habit is never repented, it can become an iniquity, increasing
the chances of it being passed to the next
generation. This is exactly what Satan wants. His evil plan is to take
advantage of family discord, unconfessed generational iniquities,
dysfunction, poor choices, sin, rejection, and whatever else he can
recycle to cause relationships to collapse. The good news is that we
are not without help and guidance. God offers a choice for us; it's a
warning along with a piece of wisdom from Deuteronomy 30:19. "I
call heaven and earth as witnesses against you today, that I have set
before you life and death, the blessing and the curse; therefore, you
shall choose life in order that you may live, you and your descen-
dants …"

We often hear that children don't come with a manual. I disagree with that. The Bible is a parent's manual, especially for their emotional well-being and for the growth of their identity. Deuteronomy 30:19 offers parents two choices: life or death. One causes a blessing, and the other reaps a curse. The Hebrew word translated "life" conveys the idea of movement. And because God desires a relationship with His created, it would behoove us to move towards Him. Likewise, we ought to move or step toward our children, whether still in the home or not. If life means "movement" towards someone, then the word "death" also means movement. Death, in this context, means to step away (Trent and Smalley 36–39).

> **The Bible is the parent's manual, especially for their children's emotional well-being and for the growth of their identity.**

From the Deuteronomy passage above, the word for curse means a "trickle" or "muddy stream" caused by a dam or obstruction upstream. When the rejecting parent speaks ill of their child, whether young or an adult, this is a curse. Parents who curse their children are choosing to "dam up the stream" by refusing life-giving actions and words that could flow down to that person (Trent and Smalley 38). Just look at the wisdom of Proverbs 18:21: "Death and life are in the power of the tongue. And those who love it and indulge it will eat its fruit and bear the consequences of their words." God gives us a choice. Either to bless or to curse. Will we step toward our children or step back? Will we choose to pour into our children's lives with good things or dam up the flow? (Trent and Smalley 38–39). Approval and acceptance help to flow "life" into our relationships. When we choose to step toward others, we are choosing God's best, His favor, and His blessings, and even life for the next generation.

CHAPTER THREE

WHAT'S IT GOING TO BE?

Behind my smile is a hurting heart.
Behind my laugh, I'm falling apart. Look closely at me,
and you will see the girl I am … isn't me.

—Unknown

"Lisa! I need you to get up and get moving!" Mama snapped as I heard her set down two breakfast bowls on the kitchen table for Davey and Timothy.

"I'm up!" I hollered.

With two little boys, Mama rose early in the mornings, and being a no-nonsense woman, she had little use for pleasantries. In much the same way as I recalled my grandfather, Mama didn't bother with a warm smile and a "good morning" or offer an affectionate hug to start the day. This made it difficult to determine her mood, something I tried to establish upon waking. She went about her days driven by a forceful energy, yet her momentum didn't come from a fountainhead of inner contentment or a stream of faith-inspired energy. Whatever its origin, it put me on edge.

One day, I came home from school to find Mama on the phone with Grandma. Engaged in another disagreement, she was madder than a hornet, yelling into the phone. This was no small squabble. She slammed the phone's receiver down, abruptly ending the quarrel. When she turned to face me, her acid anger made her entire body rigid, with her jaw squared off. She lit a cigarette and walked about our basement home ranting about her mother, highlighting her faults in between long draws on her cigarette. With no walls or doors, there was no place to disappear to and no quiet place to concentrate on homework. Whatever resentment Mama harbored towards her mother, a seed of loathing had sprouted, eclipsing her moods and personality.

Mama's temperamental disposition became agonizing to navigate. I scrutinized my own actions to avoid saying or doing something to set her off. Each word I considered speaking had to be carefully weighed against the charged atmosphere. And if I didn't meet her expectations on a household task, I faced harsh scolding.

"Young lady! What were you thinking?!" Mama would shout. Her over-the-top volatility was so intimidating that I froze in her presence, unable to put my thoughts into an explanation.

"Speak up!" Mama often yelled, glaring at me. "Quit your mumbling!"

This perceived character flaw, in which I was unable to spit my words out intelligently or at a volume she could hear, only made her more exasperated with me. When I attempted to explain myself, she became suspicious, accusing me of an ulterior motive.

Since starting high school, it became increasingly difficult to connect with Mama on any level. Her critical and judgmental nature left little room for spontaneous discussions, and unsure how she'd react to impromptu fun, I usually avoided it. I never knew just how it would be received. I couldn't risk being ridiculed. While driving to Lawrence for my weekly Campus Life meetings, I dwelled on the alarming changes I saw in Mama. While on visits with Dad in California, I asked him to explain the changes that took place in Mama's personality and demeanor back in '71 and '72 when she had a mental breakdown. Now, I was witnessing much of the same demeanor as what Dad had described. I worried Mama was relapsing.

I swung my legs off the bed and felt the cold concrete floor. Mama's added chore of watering the fruit trees distressed me. Dad was punctual. I knew he wouldn't want to spend extra time on Mama and Kevin's property waiting for me to finish my chores. Even though Dad had never spoke ill of Mama to me, she often belittled Dad in an angry lecture following a mistake I made or something I didn't do to her expectations. I put on a pair of work jeans and a clean tee shirt, then headed to the kitchen.

"Hi, Sissy," my four-year-old half-brother, Davey, said as he shoveled a spoonful of cereal into his mouth. I hugged him from behind while Timothy, in his powder blue sleeper, tilted his head back and smiled, presenting his baby teeth. I loved these boys, and my heart swelled with affection whenever they called me "Sissy."

Watering Mama's fruit trees was no simple task. The water came from the pond. Since learning to drive Kevin's antique tractor, I would drive it along the dike, pulling a small trailer that held a drum. I then used a pump to siphon water up the pond's bank through a hose into the drum.

After finishing breakfast, I left the house to do my required watering, looking forward to my visit with Dad.

As I waited for the water drum to fill, I felt the start of the penetrating heat of a Midwest summer day. Kevin's milo fields were near maturity. Their brown feathery tops swayed in unison to the morning breeze. Soon, the milo would be ready to harvest.

Kevin, a tall, quiet, even-tempered man with coal-black hair and large, black-framed eyeglasses, grew up in McAllister. His parents had a sizable farm a few miles north. He came from a large family, the youngest of five children.

My brother, Mike, and I met Kevin towards the end of the fall of '72. One night he brought Mama home after an evening out. What we didn't know was that Kevin had proposed. And Mama accepted.

When the two of them came inside, Mike and I got up from the dining room table where we were doing homework. Grandpa rose from his favorite recliner and turned down the television. Grandma finished up in the kitchen. As the grown-ups gathered in the living room making small talk, I studied Kevin's tall stature. Then my gaze went down to his large and shiny black shoes.

"You have big feet!" I blurted out, interrupting the grown-up's conversation. Everyone stopped talking, looked down at me, and immediately broke into laughter. I was embarrassed and felt awkward by the sudden attention.

Kevin leaned over. A warm smile spread across his square-shaped face; his cheeks still red from the outside chill. As he spoke, his deep voice drew out his vowels, making his words slightly elongated.

"Noo-body's ever said that to me before, but it's nice to meet you, Lisa." Though I missed Daddy, I took a liking to Kevin.

With the drum filled with water, I pulled the trailer with the drum back across the dike and over to the rows of new saplings. I found safety in the chores I knew well; they gave me a sense of confidence because I knew what to do. Trouble found me when Mama gave me a new chore with little explanation of how she wanted it done. She seemed satisfied with her instructions, yet once I began, invariably I had questions. Mama's explanations resembled Swiss cheese; they had missing information. Knowing her threshold of patience was extremely low, I grew distressed in this predicament. I could either do the task in the way I *thought* she meant or stop and go back and ask for clarification. Either option was a gamble. When I chose the latter, this usually angered her. Mama's revised instructions came with a harsh tone but also severe ridicule as punishment.

"Your problem, Lisa, is that you don't think!" Mama scolded me, thumping my forehead with her index finger and thumb. "You don't use your head!"

I unhooked the trailer with the water drum, then grabbed the long hose and extended it out to the middle of the first row of fruit trees. As I moved between the rows dispensing water, the quiet stillness of the first hours of a country morning masked the awaiting disaster.

Standing amongst the young saplings, I reflected on the last time I saw Dad. It was two months earlier at my high school graduation. Afterwards, Mama unexpectedly extended an invitation to him to join us for a small family get-together back at the house. This impromptu invitation seemed out of character for her. Given that she despised him, she was rarely civil to Dad. Even worse, she had no shame in shooting verbal arrows of bitterness at him in the presence of others. My heart wanted to enjoy that day in my honor, but it was overshadowed by the fear that, at any moment, the bottom would drop out. I couldn't trust her to behave, even with Grandpa and Grandma present, so I did what I normally did when family got together. I suppressed my inner turmoil and carried on, but inside, I could never relax or be completely present in the moment.

Under a cloud of apprehension, we assembled around the patio table, sharing a light meal. Surprisingly, the visit carried on pleasantly, but being too accustomed to family strife, I was sure this day would turn out disastrous. To my surprise, Mama remained cordial. As I opened my graduation gifts, I remained on guard but dared to hope Mama was at least a little bit proud of me.

As I watched the water flood the base of each fruit tree, I thought about my upcoming campus tour plan with Dad. When I was almost finished watering, I checked my watch. Panic gripped my heart. Where had the time gone?! For years, I could never trust Mama alone with Dad, not since the time she berated him for coming to the front door of our home in Lawrence to pick up Mike and me. From then on, I was angst-filled whenever Dad arrived. After that, he parked in the driveway and honked his horn to let us know he had arrived.

Now, if I wasn't ready, he'd have to wait. With Mama's foul mood that morning, I worried she'd be rude to him, spoiling my visit. Out of fear, I felt responsible for protecting him, but in my scattered thinking, I made a grave mistake. I hastily returned the tractor, trailer, and water drum back to the outbuilding, reasoning that I could finish watering the fruit trees on Sunday when Dad brought me back home. Little did I know, Mama's anger was already locked and loaded before I returned to the house.

"Just because your dad is in town doesn't mean you can walk out and leave me to finish your chores, young lady!" Mama shouted, her eyebrows pulled tightly together.

I shut the kitchen door behind me. Caught by surprise, I stood there in a clumsy fashion, my eyes fixed on Mama's livid face. Fear coursed its way through my body as I searched my fragmented thoughts for how to explain myself. Getting the words right was paramount, as it determined how this confrontation would go.

"I can finish the watering on Sunday when I return," I blurted out, hoping it pleased her that I didn't expect her to do my chores. Unfortunately, Mama's tone indicated she was beyond reasoning with.

"Your father can just sit and wait while you finish watering my trees," Mama ordered.

"Since this is just a short visit ... just for the weekend ...," I stammered, trailing off. Mama interrupted me, escalating into a "my house, my rules" tirade and criticizing me for not following directions. As I stood there, absorbing her anger, I realized I hadn't brushed my teeth or packed for staying with my friend, Linda, during Dad's visit. Fearing Mama would perceive any movement as defiant, I nervously eased slowly away from the door and headed to the bathroom.

Mama waited outside the bathroom door, continuing her rant, adding how she didn't care it was Dad coming. And then, Mama used her most powerful weapon—her tongue. As I applied a strip of toothpaste on my toothbrush, I heard it—words that would change the trajectory of my life.

"If you can't tell your father to wait, then you've got fifteen minutes to decide where you're going to live!"

There it was, the ultimatum I sensed had been coming for some time. Mama had agreed on the pickup time for Dad that morning, but adding the last-minute chore of watering fruit trees didn't seem reasonable. Maybe, just like my brother, Mike, my time had come to leave home, too. I was ready, even though I lacked the money for a sudden move. I was told I'd have to live at home during college because my college grant and student loan weren't enough for campus living. I accepted this, knowing it would be a challenge studying in a basement with no walls and toddlers roaming around. However, now everything seemed off the table.

My face grew hot, and I cringed under piercing stomach pains. While Mama paced between the kitchen and the bathroom, she cursed me by shouting off a list of all my unworthy traits, amplifying the weaknesses that reminded her of my dad. Fatigued, I rested my jaw in the palm of my left hand with my left elbow planted on the bathroom counter for support. I brushed my teeth with greater intensity while Mama concluded her tirade with one last criticism— that I was an ungrateful brat. Aghast, tears suddenly rushed forth. I forced them back, but they came anyway.

Unlike Kevin's milo fields that needed little water to thrive, my soul was parched. As hard as I tried, I couldn't satisfy Mama, always falling short under her critical eye. Not every day was filled with emotional abuse, but every day, I walked on eggshells, distressed on the inside. Each morning, before rising, I prayed she'd be in a good mood and that she'd be pleased with my efforts around the farm and in taking care of my young brothers.

And then a horrible realization struck me. To Mama, I was despicable. Suddenly, a weakness in my spirit came over my heart. At that moment, I knew I was done. *God*, I silently prayed, *I can't do this anymore*, was all I could say. My inner resolve plummeted. I knew I couldn't carry on this way and succeed in college.

Unaware that my elbow had gone off the edge of the counter, I nearly crashed my chin into the edge of the sink. I caught myself midway, but my body recoiled at the high-pitched crashing sound coming from the kitchen. Mama threw Davey's and Timothy's breakfast bowls into the sink, followed by more loud demeaning remarks. Her irrational actions scared me, but it also angered me that she had scared the boys. They remained in the family room and quietly played with their toys. I was done with Mama's tirade about how I was such a disappointing daughter, just like my dad had been a disappointing husband and Grandma a disappointing mother. And then I did the one thing that crossed the line with Mama. I talked back to her.

I spit out a mouthful of toothpaste, stood up, catching a quick glimpse of my distraught reflection and tear-soaked face in the mirror. I walked to the kitchen, still holding my toothbrush.

"I can finish watering the fruit trees when I get back, but if that's not good enough, then you can learn to drive the tractor like I did and water the fruit trees yourself!"

I had never dared to speak this way to Mama; nobody in my family had. Too browbeaten, I feared she'd slap me. However, for the first time, I took the risk, knowing Dad would arrive at any moment. His coming gave me a hint of empowerment. Tears continued to cascade unrestrained down my cheeks, mixing in with the toothpaste around the edges of my mouth as I contemplated Mama's likely reaction.

Surprisingly, Mama became quiet for a few moments. But I immediately knew what this was. I had seen it before in fights with Kevin. She was formulating her next verbal assault. Mama always had the upper hand, the last word, and that day was no different. Words could soar off her tongue like venom, but it was the heartless nature of those words that astounded me. She could extrapolate my reasoning with pinpoint precision and twist it into odd, deceptive judgments. I wondered how my own mother could fabricate such fallacies and assign them to me.

I raced back to the bathroom. In a frenzy, I rinsed out my mouth, still clutching my toothbrush.

"I need an answer now, young lady! Where are you going to live!?" Mama screamed. Whenever I heard the words "young lady," I knew she had crossed the line and might become physical.

Just then, I heard a car pull up outside, followed by two honks of the horn. Relief came over me, but at the same time, I worried Mama would confront Dad and order him off the farm. Back in my room, I hastily tossed a few clothing items into my duffle bag, including my toothbrush. Mama lingered around the woodstove in the center of our basement home; I figured so she could see in all directions. Ready to depart, I trembled, trying to dredge up the courage to give my answer to Mama's ultimatum. Unlike her, I couldn't think on my feet in the heat of battle. There was even a small part of me that just wanted to drop to the floor in a heap and concede and do what my family had always done—surrender. But I had seen how badly it had turned out for them. Even Kevin's children from his previous marriage no longer came to visit their dad. If I could only escape. Disappear. I didn't have it in me to fight her. And thoughts of where I'd live and how I'd pay for rent raced around my head like pinballs.

I felt backed into a corner. If I moved out, what would this mean? What unknown consequences would this bring on me? Going against Mama's demands always had long-range consequences. And what about college this fall? All I knew was that if I chose to leave, there was no turning back.

As Dad waited outside in the car and Mama waited inside, with her arms staunchly folded across her chest, tracking my whereabouts, an enormous pressure fell on me. No matter what my decision was, I knew this wasn't over; it never was with Mama. I saw Davey and Timothy sitting motionless in the carpeted family room as if they understood the gravity of the situation. Looking up at me, they too seemed to be waiting for my answer.

"Lisa!" Mama bellowed one more time. "What's it going to be?!"

CHAPTER FOUR

PEARLS AND PIGS

To love is to make of one's heart a swinging door.

—Howard Thurman

In ancient times, before fences came into existence, landowners used stones as boundary markers to designate where one person's property ended and another's began.

In the Bible, God had plenty to say about ancient boundary stones. In Deuteronomy 19:14 it says, "You shall not move your neighbor's boundary mark, which the forefathers have set, in the land which you will inherit in the land which the LORD your God is giving you to possess." When the ancient Israelites settled the Promised Land, the property was divided between families and marked with boundary stones. Today, we have land surveys in which land is plotted with legal boundary descriptions. Survey pins replaced the ancient boundary stones.

This biblical command comes up again in Proverbs 22:28. "Do not move the ancient landmark [at the boundary of the property] Which your fathers have set." In fact, it appears four other times in Scripture. (Deuteronomy 27:17; Job 24:2; Proverbs 23:10; and

Hosea 5:10). God put this command in place for a reason—to stop any encroachment on another's land. But the honor system has inherent flaws. Some landowners moved the boundary stones, adding property that wasn't theirs. In secret they moved the stone little by little over time, hoping his neighbor wouldn't notice.

But even if the neighbor didn't notice, God did. Moving a boundary stone was theft, and its shame revealed a lack of integrity.

Some years ago, I read the book *Boundaries*, by Drs. Henry Cloud and John Townsend. What I learned was pivotal.

Consider your heart like the land in those verses—your heart is your property to manage and protect. Not only does your heart dwell within *your* body, but what resides within it—*your* thoughts, emotions, desires, goals, dreams, and hopes—is also your property (Cloud and Townsend 60-68). However, like the incremental encroachment of the ancient boundary stone, toxic and rejecting parents can encroach into the property of your heart and claim unrightful ownership. And God sees that too.

> Like the incremental encroachment of the ancient boundary stone, toxic and rejecting parent(s) can encroach into the property of your heart and claim unrightful ownership.

God didn't create us with just physical bodies. We are made up of three parts: body, soul, and spirit (1 Thessalonians 5:23). Did you know that the word for "soul" is *psuche*? It's where we get our root word "psychology." This would include our intellect, our creativity, and emotions like happiness, sorrow, anger, and compassion, but also mental functions such as wonder, remembering, and reasoning. It also includes our will ("The Three Parts of Man"). These aspects of ourselves become our personality, and they belong to us. The Greek word for spirit is *pneuma* (pneuma). This part reflects our vertical relationship with God. Because of Adam and Eve's sin, our spirit became separated; however, when we become born-again Christians, that spiritual connection is restored (Colossians 1:21–22). It's through our spirit that we can be in a relationship with God.

We're aware of physical boundaries like gates and fences, but according to Cloud and Townsend, there are also spiritual boundaries. These are invisible boundaries. Harder to define, they're biblical concepts meant to safeguard what is already within one's boundary (your personal property) and to keep out what would do harm if its boundary were breached (38–39).

Emotional Encroachment

Proverbs 4:23 is an example of a spiritual boundary. "Watch over your heart with all diligence, for from it flow the springs of life." When abuse takes place in the life of a child, deep injuries happen in the bedrock of the child's soul and spirit. Like me, maybe you, too, were not aware of the stealth-like encroachment in which normal emotional and mental development was hindered. And it wasn't until you were grown that you realized you had been out of touch with various aspects of your emotional self. Childhood trauma will do that.

Boundaries are designed to keep the good in and the bad out. They guard the treasures of our hearts so others won't steal them. Doctors Cloud and Townsend sum it up this way: "They keep the pearls on the inside, and the pigs outside" (Cloud and Townsend 43).

In another book I highly recommend, *Changes that Heal*, by Dr. Henry Cloud, he states, "When we truly live in time, which is where we are now, we are present and aware of our experiences. We are present in the 'here and now.'" If we are not aware of our experience or are not experiencing some aspect of ourselves, that part is removed from time and is not affected by it. What this means is that growth can't happen in "bad time"—that is, those times of emotional stress or recurring trauma, in those areas in which we are not experiencing parts of ourselves. Change only takes place in "good time" in which our experiences are affected by grace and truth (Cloud 31–32).

There were times during my teenage years I was present in my experiences physically, but not completely on an emotional level. In a home with little grace, I was stuck in "bad time." I was inhibited, emotionally restrained from experiencing some aspects of my spirit due to the trauma of emotional manipulation and verbal abuse. Certain parts of my identity weren't being developed, such as my right to ask for what I needed. I longed for acceptance and connectivity, but my heart was locked down. I couldn't open up without fear of Mama's negative psychoanalysis, humiliation, or anger. Mama's encroachment into my heart crossed spiritual boundaries. Additionally, her toxic behavior and scapegoating led to feelings of guilt and shame, which I learned later is a Spirit of Condemnation. This spirit is the devil's way of distorting thoughts and reminding people of past mistakes and failures to make them doubt their worth and feel undeserving of God's blessings. Satan's goal is to keep you bound in a Spirit of Condemnation to limit God's working in your life.

> **Consider your childhood:**
> **Did you have adequate "good time" to develop your identity?**

Like Mama, I discovered I had boundary issues of my own; however, they were of a different kind. When Mama went ballistic, she often told me I was "the problem." Over time I internalized her assessment, and her anger and condemnation influenced my thoughts, how I viewed myself, and it controlled my behavior. Years later I learned a poignant lesson. The Lord gave me a nugget of spiritual truth: the awareness that I had taken responsibility for Mama's emotions. Whether she was enraged, irritated, or moody, they settled into my spirit, and I became ruled by them. And when she was pleasant, then I could briefly exhale. This was my boundary problem. Although I wasn't at fault, I became the scapegoat—a

> **Satan's goal is to keep you bound in a spirit of condemnation to limit God's working in your life.**

role that wasn't mine to take—for whatever wasn't working right in Mama's life. These were *her* feelings, *her* attitudes, *her* emotions, and *her* actions—all within her own boundary to control—yet she refused to own them or take responsibility for them. Mama's unbridled emotions manipulated my heart and assigned them as my emotional burdens to carry. This is the definition of a *controller*. Controllers are unable to respect others' boundaries, but it goes deeper. According to Drs. Cloud and Townsend, *aggressive controllers* are not aware that others have boundaries; neither do they respect their no (Cloud and Townsend 83). Recall from chapter two the concept of "to curse?" Being verbally abusive or not validating a child's emotions can become an obstruction that causes the flow of a child's life to become a trickle or even dammed up (Trent and Smalley 36). I can honestly say that during my teen years the flow of my life had been dammed up.

As a compliant and submissive teen, I was a suitable scapegoat for Mama for releasing the pressure of her resentments, personal disappointments, failures, and injustices. Unknowingly, I took the blame and guilt for whatever was wrong in her life. Having no understanding of how to take off the coat of guilt, let alone how to refuse to wear it in the first place, Mama had a firm grip on my heart. Stripped of the freedom to voice my own feelings, viewpoints, and emotions, I was unable to use words such as "It's not okay to criticize, threaten, or belittle me" or "I get it that you feel hurt and angry, and I care, but I am not responsible *for* it, nor should I *feel* responsible for it." In part, the Spirit of Condemnation prevented me from forming my own set of spiritual boundaries. I had to first shed the emotional burden that I was "the problem." When rejecting parents move into the territory of a child's heart in ungodly ways to conquer and manipulate, they have not only crossed a boundary, but they failed to help teach appropriate personal, emotional, physical, and spiritual boundaries to their children. After learning about spiritual boundaries, it led me to examine who I had been, but it also meant that I had to know who I'd become. What would I base my identity on? This would take many seasons of "good time."

God's intention is never for one of His children to walk around with a Spirit of Condemnation. Jesus came to set people free of such oppression. Isaiah 61:1 says, "… to proclaim release [confinement and condemnation] to the [physical and spiritual] captives …" Condemnation in our spirit is oppression. And oppressed people are controlled people. It's bondage. It's hard for a child to grow into a self-confident person when there isn't enough "good time," meaning time that is accepting and nurturing in a home that also expresses grace. Growth is stalled or halts altogether. Emotional regulation is stalled. Developing an identity is stalled. Boundaries are vague, weak, or non-existent. Even self-esteem and self-confidence are negatively affected, as was true for me. During my visits with Dad or my grandmother or friends ("good time") where grace and acceptance flowed, my true self emerged. It felt liberating. I expressed myself without fear of rejection or condemnation. I could be a more honest "me" because I had been extended grace to do so. But once back home, "good time" was suspended, and my true self went underground again.

How has your understanding of what it means to honor parents helped or hindered your relationship with them growing up?

Spiritual Fences

So how do we watch over our hearts with all diligence according to Proverbs 4:23? With a boundary—a spiritual fence. We do this by first establishing what our spiritual boundaries will be with our rejecting parent(s). For starters, begin with the words "yes" and "no." Those two small words hold power. Sadly, the dammed-up nature of my inner self prevented me from voicing my no. Without the freedom to do so, the gate of my heart was always left open for more wounding. Your yes and your no tell others what you will or won't accept. Think of your yeses and no's as boundary stones. Your yeses and no's put limits on inappropriate behavior. You have to determine what kind of behavior you'll permit from your rejecting parent(s). Remind them you are a grown-up with a separate identity with the right to have varied opinions, beliefs, and principles, and you won't tolerate judgment. If your rejecting parent continues to criticize you, you are within your boundary to respectfully ask him or her to stop. If they refuse, ask them to leave, or give yourself the permission to leave. Remember, aggressive controllers don't respect other people's boundaries, so you're not being mean. You are showing them you have regained control over your heart.

Ask yourself, "In what areas of my heart have I lost control? What types of boundaries have I not managed well or protected?" Write those down. Then make a list in advance of what types of responses your rejecting parent uses that violate the boundaries you've established. Then decide how you will respond. For example, say, "I'm not okay with you criticizing my husband," or "I'm not willing to visit or correspond if you continue to belittle me or my spouse or send hate mail."

There are consequences to a toxic and controlling parent who disrespects reasonable boundaries. Adam and Eve didn't take God seriously regarding the boundary He put forth when He instructed them to not eat the fruit of one certain tree. They opened the gate to the garden, and evil entered in. What were their consequences? They were told to leave the garden.

According to Townsend and Cloud, "Boundaries define us. They define what is me and what is *not* me. A boundary shows me where I end and someone else begins, leading me to a sense of ownership" (39). It comes down to this: What is inside my fence is mine to be responsible for, and what is inside yours is your property to manage. (38).

If we are responsible for hurting someone's feelings, intentionally or unintentionally, we should work to make amends, if possible, and restore the relationship and forgive.

To enforce our spiritual boundaries, as part of exercising our separate identity, we must establish a spiritual fence. This idea of being separate but striving to live in unity with the rejecting parent(s) is vital. God desires connectivity, but He doesn't expect us to give up our identities to do so. Hear my heart here. I remember how I melted into Mama's demands for fear that if I didn't, I'd be punished, shunned, and belittled. This fear stems from a lack of grace in the home and my own undefined boundaries, including the inability to say no. Essentially, I had lost control of what was in my heart to control. This is one reason God takes parenting seriously. Little hearts and identities are at stake. Replacing our true selves with a false self in relating to a parent who has stepped back from us is not what God asks of us. This isn't the definition of honoring our parents. Presenting a false self tells the rejecting parent that you are weak, and they can lord their power over you and continue to intrude and violate your heart. Their continued encroachment has the potential to inflict injury, potentially stopping or blocking the life that flows from your soul and spirit (Proverbs 4:23). We must be true to God and ourselves first before we can show our true selves to others.

A Spiritual Gate

Establishing healthy boundaries brings value and protection to our lives. But our spiritual fences need gates. A gate serves two purposes: It will keep the bad from getting in, but it also allows the good that others have to offer to pour in (Cloud and Townsend 75). It allows for protection but also for blessing. Think of it as opening the gate to release what will poison our hearts so that God can in return dispense truth, discernment, grace, and blessing to our souls. As you'll see in my story, I didn't have the knowledge back then about establishing a spiritual fence. This is because of an undefined identity. As a result, this set me up to be emotionally wounded over and over. You may see yourself in some of my experiences, but thankfully, God does intervene and sets me on a new course. He takes me on a journey to find my true self, while revealing the work of distortion Satan so cleverly sowed. If I could use one word that became the master key to freedom, it's truth.

CHAPTER FIVE

THE DECISION

Choices are the hinges of destiny.

—Pythagoras

If I didn't say the words now, it was doubtful I ever would. With my purse over my shoulder and my duffel bag in my hand, I cut across the family room to put some distance between Mama and me.

"Where are you going, Sissy?" Davey shyly asked, looking up at me.

His question caught me off guard. My gut wrenched for my young half-brothers. Conflicted, part of me desperately wanted to escape, but leaving them in this awful way burdened my heart even more. I wanted to take them into my arms and whisper an assuring word: *I'll always be your Sissy,* but Mama's seething anger propelled me to keep moving.

"I'm going to town, but I'll see you later," I promised, trying to force a smile. Regrettably, I didn't know when I'd see them again.

I stood with my back against the kitchen door with my left hand behind me nervously twisting the doorknob, trying to muster the courage to speak the words I had to say. Mama's eyes bored into mine from across the kitchen.

For a moment, her eyes locked with mine, changing from bright blue to dark and piercing, with a livid expression of contempt. It gave me a spine-chilling sensation, making me think of demonization. The thought seemed preposterous, yet there was something threatening about her countenance. I couldn't detect the slightest hint of light or warmth behind them.

"I guess I need to find a new place to live," I muttered, relieved to get the words out, yet fearing her coming reaction. I wasn't expecting what came next.

"Good! Because I can't stand the sight of you!" Mama screamed, shaking her fist at me. "We're going camping this weekend. I want you and your things out of the house by the time we get back!"

She turned away, walked a few steps, then quickly whipped back to face me again. Again, I knew what this was. I had seen it before when she argued with Kevin and Grandma. It was her last say. Her crescendo of all crescendos, meant to impale my heart.

"And that includes your damn cat!" Mama ordered.

I stood looking at her in disbelief. I had forgotten about Jody. Mama's cruelty gutted me, leaving me speechless. I picked up my duffel bag, then turned and walked out. Heading towards Dad's rental car, my whole body felt weak, my legs like jelly. Hearing the kitchen door open, I didn't dare look; I kept walking. And then I felt it. Something hit the back of my head. A dull pain ensued. Mama had found my hairbrush I had left on a cabinet beside the door and hurled it at me. I picked it up, catching a quick glance at her, noting her look of disdain as she retreated back inside the house.

All it took was one look at me, and Dad knew what happened. "Fight with your mother?"

"Hi, Dad," I managed to say, brushing the tears off my face. We both leaned into one another to exchange a hug.

"I have to find a place to live," I confessed, relieved that Mama hadn't followed me out to the car. Dad took a moment to contemplate the situation.

"I'm sorry," he said, sighing. "And did she throw something at you?"

"Yeah, my hairbrush. She actually has good aim; she hit me in the head."

I could see the disgust on Dad's face as he shook his head.

He put the car in reverse. "And that's not all. I have to find a new home for Jody." The tears began to flow again. It hurt deeply to contemplate what would become of him.

Mama knew this would punch me hard in my already beat-up heart. I dreaded having to tell Grandma this awful news. At a time when I was a depressed eleven-year-old, I had needed Jody as much as he needed me. I *still* needed him.

"I'm sorry about your cat, hon," Dad offered. "You know how I like cats, but I'm only here until Sunday. For now, let's get to Lawrence and find a place for you to live."

Except for the hard, crunching sound of the car traveling over gravel, we sat quietly, although I was still trembling inside. I knew Dad was giving me some space. I contemplated Mama's irrational behavior. Her scornful look and her heartless words, "I can't stand the sight of you!" reverberated in my head. Mama had summed me up as a pathetic daughter. Her disparaging words were not only cruel but felt malicious.

I rolled the car window down and let the morning air hit my face. Green pastures, old barns, and cows whirled by. Together with the hurt, a part of me felt a sliver of relief. But even having the inevitable over with, the relief was yoked with guilt. Was it wrong to stand up for myself and state my feelings? If not, why didn't I feel vindicated? Why did I still feel guilt-ridden? It's as if the tentacles of Mama's contempt had reached into the rental car, striking my heart. My whole being felt sick.

"So, what happened this morning?" Dad interjected, breaking into the silence.

"I didn't finish watering Mama's fruit trees, and she went ballistic."

Dad squinted his eyebrows together into a confused look. "She kicked you out because you didn't finish watering?"

"It was more of an ultimatum. I made a judgment call, and apparently, it was the wrong one."

"What kind of judgment call?"

As we drove into Lawrence, I recounted the whole painful story to Dad. "You didn't do anything wrong, hon," he reassured me. "It's not you." Those three words Dad spoke would eventually become the truth I would fight for years to rise above.

Dad's words were comforting, but Mama's relentless criticism over the years hollowed out my spirit. I felt like a failure, incapable of doing anything right. I had little self-confidence, and my emotions lay bare and tender. Even the way I styled my hair became a bone of contention between us. I struggled with my wavy, frizzy hair, but Mama simply criticized it. Like the common clematis flower, when stepped on, I stayed crumbled on the inside. It was lost to me how to win her approval. Simply being me didn't cut it.

"You're not the problem here," Dad reiterated. "I understand your difficulty with your mother; I had similar issues. Just remember, this isn't about you. And I'm sorry you've had to deal with this."

I had never shared my emotional turmoil with anyone, not even with friends, because I didn't trust Mama. Her prickly temperament and unpredictability made it risky to admit to any abuse. I knew she had it in her to retaliate. Once, when Mike and I were scheduled to fly out to California for a visit with Dad, she refused to take Mike and me to the airport. She stated she didn't have gas money, but instead of asking Dad to add gas money to his child support payemt, or send a check, she not only didn't put us on our flight, but she purposely didn't tell Dad we weren't coming. He showed up at the airport gate to discover we weren't on the plane.

I feared other repercussions, like being barred from school functions, losing my car, or seeing friends. I couldn't risk losing those; they were my emotional reprieve and kept me going. To me, Mama was a pharaoh—all powerful. And my compliant nature was to always appease the pharaoh. In actuality, I was suppressing a part of my identity that needed to be expressed. Looking back, even the adults couldn't subdue Mama's acidic anger, irrational behavior, and eventual bitterness. In retrospect, Mama lacked healthy relationships. Grandma became worried for Mama, but when she lovingly suggested professional help, Mama took it as a personal attack, insisting we were the sick ones. Unfortunately, no one ever held Mama accountable for her injurious behavior. And so, I kept my head down and did as I was told.

"She really resents you," I told Dad, "especially when you come to visit. Her demeanor changes. She's agitated and short-tempered, especially with me."

Dad's expression seemed to convey he was contemplating the situation. "Do you have any ideas of where to look for a place to live?" Dad asked, redirecting our conversation to the urgent need.

"I do, actually. Can we stop by the office of the Campus Christian House?"

"What's that?" Dad asked, as we arrived in Lawrence.

"It's a co-ed home for Christian college students attending the university. I learned about it through Campus Life in high school. There are two houses, one for the men and one for the women."

Dad knew about Campus Life. I had shared my involvement with this high school ministry with him during my visits. It became a place of emotional refuge where I could relax, knowing I wasn't being censored or judged. Weekly, I looked forward to the meetings, where for a couple of hours I received a spiritual refueling, not only for the inner strength I needed at home but for my own emotional sanity. But, at seventeen years old, I was a naïve Christian. Although I prayed God would soften Mama's heart, it hadn't occurred to me that she had to *want* that too. Just like when Jesus asked the blind man in Mark 10:51, "What do you want me to do for you?" The blind man replied, "I want to see!" From my purview, Mama seemed more interested in hurting others than seeking healing for herself.

Thank goodness, we have a God who sees what's ahead but also knows what we'll need before we even ask. He foresaw my difficult path and provided strong spiritual roots through Campus Life and later Campus Christians as a college student. During high school, I eagerly anticipated the week-long summer retreats to the mountains of Colorado. There's a mysterious element about being out in nature that turns our hearts to ponder on the awesomeness of God that deepens our spiritual relationship. Of course, walking the mountain trails, I couldn't escape thoughts of my strained relationship with Mama. Why, of all the mothers in the world, was mine set against me? I prayed, telling God how wounded and rejected I felt. I pleaded for God to change Mama's heart. But upon returning home, Mama was still Mama. Instead, God spiritually refreshed and strengthened *my* heart with His promises. I trusted in Philippians 4:13: "I can do all things through Him who strengthens and empowers me [to fulfill His purposes]." Even when I neither felt it nor saw any signs of things changing, I was learning to hang my heart on the truth that God was still in control of my circumstances and saw me and saw my silent struggle and woundedness.

Still, trusting God with Mama was tough. There were times I wanted a visible sign or a way of escape like God had done for certain people in the Bible. I wanted my own parting of the Red Sea. God always has a plan, but He isn't impulsive. He sees the end from the beginning and knows what's needed in the middle—trust and patience, with expectant waiting. Looking back, God had heard me. I realized Dad's visit that weekend *was* my way of escape. I had won my physical freedom on Independence Day, but emotional healing would be a long way off. Still, there are no coincidences for the Christian. Proverbs 16:9 says, "A man's mind plans his way, but the Lord directs his steps and establishes them." Without Dad there, I may have conceded to Mama's ultimatum.

"Since it's summer, there might be a room available in the women's Campus Christian House because most of the out-of-town college students return home for the summer," I explained to Dad. He liked the idea of me living with other college students. To him, it seemed like a good fit.

"Did you want to stop in and visit your grandparents?"

"Yeah, I'd like that. I'm sure Mama has already called Grandma and given her an earful about our fight."

I was thankful that my grandparents had maintained a good relationship with my dad. Even years after my parents' divorce, Grandma talked fondly of him. They recognized Dad had tried to keep his family together. They knew how difficult Mama could be, especially during those hard years with her nervous breakdown and her prickly demeanor. They remained cordial to Dad, a fact that probably annoyed Mama greatly. This was confirmed in an entry I read in my grandmother's journal I later received.

Yesterday was Pete's birthday. What relation is an ex-son-in-law? It makes no difference. He is almost like a real son. I sent a late birthday card.

December 22, 1979

Dad and I met with Mr. Graham, the director of Campus Christians, who understood my urgent need for housing. Thankfully, there was a vacancy. As I filled out the paperwork, Mr. Graham explained the organization's purpose and how the program would operate once the fall semester started. He explained that the Campus Christians organization had sold the two separate houses to purchase a large, three-story former fraternity house near the campus. My name was added to the list, not only securing my housing for the last month before the start of fall classes, but my living situation was set for my entire freshman year of college!

Dad paid my rent through September until my college grant and school loan would come through. In the meantime, I continued to work as a waitress at the soda fountain in the rear of Raney's Drug Store, a job Linda's mother, the manager, offered me when I was in the ninth grade. It was a nostalgic, vintage-era place with round red stools along the counter and a single row of six booths. As the local watering hole, it was a popular place known for its friendly and casual style. Every Saturday morning, the same senior menfolk converged upon the soda fountain, my grandfather included, to discuss politics, football, and the economy. It was here, in the soda fountain, where I had the pleasure of serving my grandfather and where I witnessed the good-natured side of him.

Mr. Graham handed me the house keys. I immediately called Linda and Theresa. They graciously agreed to help me move my things out of Mama and Kevin's home that weekend.

* * * * * *

Knowing Mama's blatant hostility towards Dad, he thought better of returning to the farm to help us girls. Riding with Linda the following morning to the farm, we crested the top of the driveway. The unfinished rambler nestled in the holler popped into view. My stomach ached in distress, fearing Mama and Kevin hadn't left for camping. Relieved to find no one home, the farm felt off-putting, as if I had been exiled from both it and my family's lives. I unlocked the door and let my friends enter first. I felt like an intruder in someone else's home.

Over the next hour, my friends and I quickly gathered all my possessions, except for the heavy furniture, and loaded them into our cars, saving room for my antique steamer trunk, a gift from Mama just after she and Kevin married and during a time she was doing better. Mama found it at a garage sale.

"It would make a great hope chest," I remember Mama saying. "I'll show you how to refurbish it."

Mama and I picked out new wallpaper with a floral background and tiny yellow roses. I spent a weekend removing the old liner, sanding the wooden top shelf, measuring, and cutting the wallpaper to size, then gluing it to the interior. Proud of my hard work, I set the trunk at the foot of my bed and filled it with school memorabilia, yearbooks, photo albums, souvenirs from trips abroad, and letters from Dad. The trunk symbolized a period when I was coming out of depression, had friends, a more stable home life, and my cat, Jody. Life was better because Mama was better.

Loaded up, I returned to the house for one last look, wishing I could tell my young brothers I was leaving only the house, not their lives. I feared they'd forget me, especially if Mama didn't welcome me back. I worried she'd speak ill of me in their presence. I hoped they wouldn't forget how I read to them, pulled them through the snow on their sleds, pushed them in their swings, and took them to their favorite park with the antique steam train. I feared those memories would likely remain only with me.

Standing beside Davey and Timothy's small beds with their toys on the floor brought fresh tears. It felt like a piece of my heart broke off. Mama once said I was jealous of them. I didn't understand why she'd think that. I adored them. And I worried about them. I placed my house key on the kitchen table and locked the door on my way out. I left without looking back. The place I had lived felt cursed with no hope of ever producing warmth or blessing, at least not for me. Leaving home was supposed to be a joyful milestone in a young person's life, but in Mama's home, joy didn't have a chance. I didn't belong here—and maybe I never did.

I had my physical freedom now, yet my heart ached without Mama's blessing. This ache would remain with me for many years, always reminding me of the dissonance between us. That evening, after moving my things into my new room at the Campus Christian House, I thanked my dad and friends for their help with pizza delivery and pop. It wasn't the weekend Dad and I had planned, but I was grateful he was there. On a warm, muggy Kansas evening, we took our pizza and pop to the front porch. With the move finished and in supportive company, we ate and discussed the day. For the first time, Mama had no idea where I was or how to find me.

CHAPTER SIX

A Spirit of Rejection

*Rejection doesn't mean you aren't good enough; it means
the other person failed to notice what you have to offer.*

—Mark Amend

A s Christians, we battle against evil forces that seek to darken our minds and spirits. Satan exploits our weaknesses, mistakes, vulnerabilities, and sins, finding opportunities to sow negative emotions and false thoughts. One such tool of Satan's is a spirit of rejection. An oppressive tool, it aims to prevent Christians from experiencing freedom in Christ.

I've had many years to reflect on the cloak of darkness that blanketed my home. At the time, I was too young to understand how Satan works, but today I see things more clearly. With a more mature spiritual lens, I now understand that dark spiritual forces were at work in my home. Believers are guided by the Holy Spirit and face off against the spiritual forces of Satan and his fallen angels and demons. They work in the unseen realm in opposition to the Holy Spirit and Christians. Ephesians 6:12 says, "For our struggle is not against flesh and blood [contending with only physical opponents], but against the rulers, against the powers, against the world forces of this [present] darkness, against the spiritual forces of wickedness in the heavenly places."

Unbelievers, however, lack the presence of the Holy Spirit, but Satan has an agenda for them as well. His intention is to influence the lives of unbelievers to keep them "worldly minded." To understand a spirit of rejection, we must first understand the nature of footholds and strongholds and the role they play in giving our hearts and minds over to this destructive spirit.

Footholds—Satan's Entry Point

A foothold is a precursor to a stronghold. Today, we associate a foothold as something we place our foot on to gain support before advancing up a steep hill. In biblical Greek, it carries the same meaning but expands to include such things as position, occasion, condition, region, place, and opportunity (Neil). In the unseen world, there is much going on. Satan uses weapons such as deception, bitterness, jealousy, anger, pride, fear, and other vulnerabilities to gain a foothold in our thought life. He knows actions follow what we allow into our minds. But what does it mean when the devil gets a foothold into our lives?

The nature of a foothold is historically a military strategy. During World War II, the Allied forces used it to clinch the victory in Europe. They arrived on the beaches of Normandy and secured their position behind enemy lines (The Crossing Church). It's a strategy that works.

Another analogy is to picture someone being chased. This person runs to a room and tries to close the door, but the antagonist places his shoe at the bottom of the door so it can't be closed. The antagonist has gained a "foothold" (Cachila). God has wired us with a unique ability to sense the devil's pull in our lives. This is the point at which we can shut the door before a foothold can be established. Take for example, the insight of James 1:19 to prevent a foothold of

> Like an alligator that glides undetected beneath the water, Satan, too, prefers a stealth-like approach.

anger: "… let everyone be quick to hear [be a careful, thoughtful listener], slow to speak [a speaker of carefully chosen words and], slow to anger [patient, reflective, forgiving]."

Ephesians 4:26 offers the solution. "… do not let your anger last until the sun goes down." James isn't saying that anger is wrong, but we are not to be "quick-tempered" (Chinn). God imposes this time restraint to prevent anger from leading us into sin. It helps to break the foothold of anger.

Neglecting or willfully choosing to not manage our negative thoughts and emotions gives Satan the latitude to dangerously influence us, impacting our lives. Like an alligator that glides undetected beneath the water, Satan, too, prefers a stealth-like approach.

Second Corinthians 10:5 instructs us to "take every thought and purpose captive to the obedience of Christ," meaning we confront and willingly turn over our negative thought life to Christ. Though challenging, we have the help of the Holy Spirit. He'll help us to shift our focus to godly thinking through the renewal of our minds by His Word (Romans 12:2). Our bodies are a "living sacrifice" set apart (Romans 12:1). It includes committing to His use of our minds, mouths, wills, emotions, hands, etc. (Meyer 1665). By making this sacrifice, we hold onto the truth that Jesus rewards the obedient.

Sadly, many, including believers, fail to align with God's Word, allowing Satan to establish a foothold. Once he has created his base camp, Satan then strategizes how to take us to the next level—to a stronghold.

Strongholds—An Enslaving Lie

Dr. Mark Bubeck, pastor, founder, and president of Deeper Walk International, defines a stronghold as:

... an idea, belief, fear, feeling, desire, or anything else (arguments, pretensions against the knowledge of God) that has a strong hold, or a firm grip on, our mind, spirit, body, or heart—enslaving us—motivating us to act out against God's will through repeated sinful behavior. A stronghold is a believed lie we have allowed to become reality to us and hold us in bondage to sin. It's a lie that has darkened our minds to the truth of Christ.

A stronghold is just that—a stronghold on the heart. It's a metaphorical reference based on the walls surrounding ancient cities to keep out the enemy. In fact, the Greek word for stronghold is "fortress." Some examples of a stronghold include anger, bitterness, unforgiveness, pride, rebellion, people-pleasing, hard-heartedness, deception, or habitual sin, such as lying, pornography, or addiction—all of which come from our enemy for evil intentions. If the strongholds within us remain fortified, we're giving Satan permission to work unhindered in our hearts. A foothold gets Satan in the door—with a stronghold he sets up camp.

> **The Greek word for stronghold is "fortress."**

From this position, he seeks to take more ground. Like the ancient fortresses, these strongholds appear invincible. Don't underestimate our enemy. Satan is calculating and cunning, using our circumstances to obstruct truth and negatively affect our emotions and thinking. Consider Beth Moore's words on generational strongholds from her Bible study, Breaking Free:

We tend to think of generational hand-me-down baggage as part of who we are rather than how we're bound. In many cases, we grew up with these chains, so they feel completely natural. We're apt to consider them part of our personalities rather than a yoke squeezing abundant life out of us ... anything passed down to us that inhibits the full expression of freedom we should have in Christ qualifies as bondage. (75).

Satan has long studied the weaknesses and vulnerabilities of previous generations, closely watching for genetically predisposed behaviors and mindsets. He tirelessly plants harmful words and thoughts in our minds to weaken our spiritual muscles—such as "I've been this way for so long I can't change," and "I don't have a problem; this is who I am," or "I'm not good enough to ever achieve my dreams." We may even find excuses to justify failure. This is the devil's mission—to deceive with a lie. If you have a dream, Satan will intensify his efforts to plant defeat, using fear, uncertainty, and doubt to block you. This is why surrounding ourselves with other believers can inspire and encourage us to pursue our goals and spiritual gifts.

A complacent stance on Satan's tactics ignores John 10:10's warning that "the thief comes to steal, kill, and destroy." Satan hates believers and aims to ruin their lives and render them ineffective as Christians by keeping them bound in strongholds. Looking back, I can see I had a stronghold of fear and, in order to win Mama's approval, a stronghold of people-pleasing.

A Spirit of Rejection—An Emotional Fortress

A spirit of rejection, also known as an "orphan spirit," makes us feel unworthy and undeserving, stealing our identity, competence, opportunities, and joy. It can also trap individuals in pride and rebellion, isolating them in darkness and resisting God's truth and freedom. For believers, a spirit of rejection can blind us to God's truth. What is a real tragedy is that they're isolated in a mental and emotional prison. Later, when older, I realized Mama was bound in an emotional prison.

Despite being chosen and entrusted with God's covenant, the ancient Israelites, in their rebellion against God, were blind and deaf to God's direction. As a result of their disobedience, they ended up suffering and in captivity. Look at what Isaiah 42:22-23 says of His people:

But this is a people despoiled and plundered; All of them are
trapped in holes,
Or are hidden away in prisons.
They have become prey with no one to rescue them,
And a spoil, with no one to say, "Give them back!"

Because of their rebellion and refusal to carry out their covenant with God, there was no one to fight for them. Like an animal out in the open, unprotected, they became Satan's prey. They found themselves alone and isolated. It is the same today. People bound up in strongholds are like prey with no one to rescue them. No one to say, "Give them back!"

A spirit of rejection can also be inherited through generations. Mama's life was marked by strongholds rooted in her father's early years. My grandfather was born in 1918. His father forced his wife to give my grandfather away to another family at the tender age of two, leaving him with a lifetime mysterious void. As an adult, my grandfather made many attempts to find his biological family, but sadly he died never knowing who they were or the circumstances that led to being rejected and later abandoned by his father. Upon learning this, I made the correlation that rejection by a parent had likely become a generational curse in my family, going back three generations.

What I do know about my great-grandfather was that he was a temperamental and demanding man, as was my grandfather. By no means was my grandfather a conversationalist, but when he did have something to say, it often was to prove a point. And when he did, it often came down forcefully. Growing up, his unpredictable moods made me uneasy. He had never been unkind to me, but he wasn't easily approachable. And because of his seemingly sour disposition, I seldom saw him smile. On the surface, it seemed his grumpy and temperamental side was an inherited trait. Strongholds can be hard to recognize. To my grandfather, his anger problem may have been explained as a hand-me-down trait, figuring it was simply part of his personality, however, it's plausible he was bound in a spirit of rejection, especially since this trait was passed down to his two children, my mother and her brother, Robert. Severed relationships as well as abandonment as a child can genetically predispose us to a spirit of rejection. Like her father, my mother's difficult and irritable demeanor made it hard to get to know her on a personal level. I contemplated that home life for my mother and her brother, Robert, was contentious growing up. But what was behind the root of bitterness Mama had towards her mother? And now me?

Reflecting back to those difficult years at home, I now see that Satan had moved to the next generation—mine. I had been a captive of a spirit of rejection. Mama's critical demeanor led me to believe something was wrong with me, and I became performance-driven, striving to be the perfect daughter to earn her approval. Operating in this dysfunctional way opened me up for attack.

A spirit of rejection clouded my dreams and self-belief. Although I hoped to be a school teacher, fear of failure and a lack of confidence became a barrier to that goal. I didn't have a firm direction in life. Two demonic spirits, doubt and fear,

> If God placed a dream in your heart, protect it with prayer.

worked in tandem. They so pervaded my heart that I put little stock into my own dreams. Mama's home was dominated by negative energy with a pessimistic mindset about dreams. If I dared to mention my dreams, I anticipated ridicule and a lecture about being unrealistic. To Mama, dreams were far-fetched notions.

While determined not to end up angry like Mama, I battled with another facet of rejection—the stunting of my identity. Narcissistic parents who use emotional abuse strip their children of their individuality and creativity and stifle their autonomy. They inhibit their children's right to think, feel, and have their own personhood.

When we don't treat emotional wounds, they have the potential to become a breeding ground for Satan's other demons to spoil our lives and steal our joy. The author and overseer of Crusaders Ministries, John Eckhardt, states in his book, *Destroying the Spirit of Rejection*:

> *Rejection is a demon. In the rejection cluster of demons, various evil spirits come together, strengthening and deepening the enemy's hold on an individual's life ... demons behave like gangs. They operate with strategy and prowl upon people who have been made vulnerable because of emotional pain. They are drawn to weakness and especially to people struggling with rejection. (45).*

Just like a wounded wild animal, those with a spirit of rejection become an easy target for the enemy. He advances his work by using our heart wounds to inflict other demonic spirits. According to Eckhardt, some of these include insecurity, low self-confidence, depression, perfectionism, pride, fear, paranoia, indecision, passivity, guilt, and excessive sensitivity (Eckhardt 45–51).

> Whereas, the Spirit of Condemnation is Satan's tool to remind us of our past mistakes, sins, and failures to keep us stuck, a Spirit of Rejection is his tool to keep believers from experiencing liberty in Christ.

A spirit of rejection can blind us to the freeing truth of Scripture. For years, I struggled to understand 2 Corinthians 10:4, which felt like a riddle to me. It says: "The weapons of our warfare are not physical [weapons of flesh and blood]. Our weapons are divinely powerful for the destruction of fortresses."

Back then, I didn't understand what "the destruction of fortresses" meant. Strongholds, a component of a spirit of rejection, and anything that hinders us from living fully in Christ become like fortresses that keep us in bondage. They represent areas where Satan has gained victory over us, causing us to operate from a mindset of defeat.

But Satan doesn't have the final say. God has given us weapons, not worldly weapons, but divinely powerful weapons—faith, prayer, God's promises, His Word, and worship. The Greek meaning for powerful is "mighty." Because He desires for us to conquer strongholds and areas of bondage, He doesn't give us mediocre weapons. These are *mighty* weapons!

For years, I believed I was battling Mama in the physical sense, but the real fight was against her own demons and strongholds. Unaware that I was in a spiritual battle with Satan, I failed to recognize him as the true enemy, blinded by my own spirit of rejection. Eckhardt describes Satan's work as insidious. "Instead of operating in the truth of God, a person is bound and controlled by counterfeit spirits. Fear and its manifestations become a stronghold in the life of a person who carries the spirit of rejection" (Eckhardt 45).

The good news is that God's power supersedes Satan's. When Christians deploy God's divine weapons, trusting the battle to God's strength and ability, strongholds crumble, and darkness is broken. Consider what God does to the stronghold of pride in Isaiah 25:11-12. "... but the Lord will humiliate his pride in spite of the [skillful] movements of his hands. The high fortifications of your walls He will bring down, lay low, and cast to the ground, to the dust."

God not only destroys strongholds but grinds them into dust. While God has a plan for your life (Jeremiah 29:11), the devil's plan is to keep you bound by strongholds and a spirit of rejection. To overcome this, we must first recognize the spiritual battle for our souls and identify who we truly are.

We Are Warriors

Christians are warriors. And what do warriors do? We fight! Paul says in 2 Timothy 2:4: "No soldier in active service gets entangled in the [ordinary business] affairs of civilian life; [he avoids them] so that he may please the one who enlisted him to serve."

As soldiers for Christ, we're called to live lives that honor God. He has provided us with spiritual armor (Ephesians 6:10-17) to fight the spiritual battle, but we must use it. The sword of the Spirit, God's Word, represents His power, protection, and authority against strongholds. Hebrews 4:12 says:

For the word of God is living and active and full of power [making it operative, energizing, and effective]. It is sharper than any two-edged sword, penetrating as far as the division of the soul and spirit [the completeness of a person], and of both joints and marrow [the deepest parts of our nature], exposing and judging the very thoughts and intentions of the heart.

To demolish strongholds, we weigh our patterns of living and core beliefs against God's Word. Are we feeding lies to the flesh or truth to the spirit? Like Jesus did in Matthew 4, we should counter Satan's lies with Scripture, speaking life when he speaks death. For example: "A soothing tongue [speaking words that build up and encourage] is a tree of life" (Proverbs 15:4a). Because God's Word is active and alive, it can expose what is false. It rightly divides truth from lies. When we ask, God will expose the false and reveal the truth. God's truth guides us out of the pit of darkness.

Additionally, any good soldier knows his enemy. Familiarize yourself with Satan's cunning tactics. You may even notice he uses the same scheme over and over in your life because it works. He has found your vulnerabilities. Learn to overcome that area to stop Satan's assault. Part of overcoming a spirit of rejection is cultivating our faith. Finally, be encouraged by Philippians 2:12b. "… continue to work out your salvation [cultivate it, bring it to full effect, actively pursue spiritual maturity] …"

As we grow spiritually, we'll be better discerners of Satan's schemes. Unfortunately, many Christians today are complacent, making it hard to recognize his insidious work and lies. Without pursuing spiritual growth, they remain stuck in a spirit of rejection.

Evaluate Your Life

By examining our emotional wounds, we can bring these issues into the light of God's presence for prayer, revelation, healing, and restoration. Ask God to reveal your vulnerabilities, any rebellious ways, and ask Him to enhance your spiritual discernment. When I concentrated on my own healing, I prayed for discernment of my past, too. When I began to seriously study God's Word, that greater understanding started to flow into my life. I asked God to make me aware of the areas that made me vulnerable. And He did. A person who possesses a spirit of rejection tends to be highly sensitive, and any type of criticism, even if it is constructive and done in love for my benefit, I internalized as rejection. Today, I still consider myself "sensitive," but I don't internalize it as rejection. I believe God made me the way I am, sensitive, but for a purpose. My sensitivity is used to reach those who are fragile in spirit because of rejection or emotional invalidation. However, I still went on a quest to learn why I struggled with constructive criticism. I read extensively books by Christian counselors and therapists and studied spiritual concepts that pertained to my type of bondage. As I gained new understanding, the Lord opened my eyes to more. This understanding began to renew my mind, changing my thought patterns for the better. I also took courses through the American Association of Christian Counselors (AACC) to understand different aspects of how trauma affects the brain, body, and emotions, but also how demonic spirits can wreak havoc in our lives, setting us up as prey for Satan. As you read, you'll learn some of these principles that helped in my healing. One word of concern, be wary of worldly solutions because they are "maintenance programs" that teach us to keep ourselves from falling by our own wisdom, discipline, and power. They can be helpful in a secondary way but should never be offered as the primary solution. Here are several ways to prevent strongholds from gaining the ground of your heart (Foster).

Change Your Focus

Focusing on our strongholds amplifies them and reinforces emotional barriers, darkening our world and perpetuating a spirit of rejection. Instead, we should direct our focus and hearts toward Jesus. Matthew 6:22–23 says,

> *The eye is the lamp of the body; so if your eye is clear [spiritually perceptive], your whole body will be full of light [benefiting from God's precepts]. But if your eye is bad [spiritually blind], your whole body will be full of darkness [devoid of God's precepts]. So if the [very] light inside you [your inner self, your heart, your conscience] is darkness, how great and terrible is that darkness!*

Our eyes perceive the world around us and shape our perceptions. Focusing on what is spiritually positive fills us with His light while fixating on strongholds and their negativity brings darkness and distorts our thinking, impairing our ability to spiritually discern. What we allow our eyes to focus on and internalize will affect our souls.

Pray

Did you know that the fastest way to change things in our lives is through prayer and not through human manipulation? Prayerlessness is a major problem among Christians today. Neglecting this spiritual weapon weakens us against deception. Prayer is God's defense system (Phillips 25). It's the channel that allows God's grace and protection to flow into our lives. In prayer, ask the Holy Spirit to teach you to recognize the schemes of the enemy, "… so that you may be able to [successfully] stand up against all the schemes and the strategies and the deceits of the devil" (Ephesians 6:11b). God's Word is alive and active and can bring breakthroughs during spiritual attacks.

Seek a Christian Counselor

If a stronghold is too deeply embedded, or you don't know where to start, seek a certified licensed Bible counselor. One reputable online resource is www.betterhealth.com.

Referring to the nature of strongholds, Dale Johnson, who serves as Executive Director of the Association of Certified Biblical Counselors, states:

> *If we interpret and listen to the story of a person's life from the perspective simply of the flesh, it's not that we dismiss what's going on in a person's life, but if we just engage in that person's life from what we can see in a fleshly sense, we will dismiss divine power, which is able to destroy strongholds within us. That's where spiritual warfare comes in. (Johnson)*

We live in the flesh, but strongholds are fought and destroyed in the spirit realm (2 Corinthians 10:3–4). If we were to use human weapons to demolish demonic spirits, our weapons would be inadequate. We must use God's weapons because we are not fighting a human war but a spiritual war. Counseling without the spiritual aspect only addresses what we are aware of, missing the unseen spirit realm—the strongholds and the effects of a spirit of rejection, as well as God's divine power to destroy them.

Praise and Thanksgiving

First Thessalonians 5:18 encourages us to be thankful in all circumstances, not for them. Praise often moves God and changes lives, but a spirit of thankfulness can be elusive when facing rejection and strongholds. Daily oppression from parental rejection can wear down our souls. We wonder if God really sees us. Psalm 34:15 says He does. "The eyes of the LORD are toward the righteous and His ears are open to their cry." Hope and confidence in God are what anchor our soul for difficult seasons.

Remember Job's wife? She was so distraught by one tragic blow after another that she completely gave up on God. You could say she pulled her anchor up in defeat. She limited God's ability to restore all that she had lost. In fact, she told her husband, Job, "Curse God and die!" (Job 2:9b). Her once thankful heart was replaced by a spirit of bitterness. Our enemy would prefer that we succumb to defeat like Job's wife. But when maintaining an attitude of thankfulness, it strengthens us and increases our spiritual resolve to overcome Satan's schemes.

Job's wife, often criticized for her lack of faith, reminds us that repeated loss and adversity can weaken our faith. Her desire for relief reflects the limits of our humanity. I empathize with her. Although God is sovereign and allows circumstances beyond our understanding, maintaining our confidence in Him and staying in faith—rather than abandoning hope—will allow us to witness His work.

Indeed! God does see us! He sees our wounded hearts and woos us to Himself. And He sees us as overcomers. Hebrews 10:35–36 tells us why:

> Do not, therefore, fling away your [fearless] confidence, for it has a glorious and great reward. For you have need of patient endurance [to bear up under difficult circumstances without compromising], so that when you have carried out the will of God, you may receive and enjoy to the full what is promised.

God aims to break rejection and strongholds, and if we maintain fearless confidence in Him, He promises us a rewarding outcome to enjoy. Lastly, be encouraged, "resist him [Satan], be firm in your faith ..." (1 Peter 5:9a).

CHAPTER SEVEN

A Sapphire of Hope

A lot of my favorite childhood memories with my grandparents are not stored in photos but in certain biscuits, warm hugs, smells, and textures of carpet.

—Proud Happy Mama

A t barely five feet tall, Grandma and I could look each other in the eye. Meticulous about her appearance, Grandma put herself together as if she were still working. Daily she wore a polyester-knit fitted dress, accentuating her adorably plump figure. I never saw Grandma in pants of any kind, ever. She told me once that she tried on a pair of gaucho-style slacks at a department store. She chuckled as she began to describe how she looked in the wide-legged trousers. All of a sudden, her chuckle turned into a belly laugh, and the only word I could make out was "hideous!" My imagination got the best of me when I envisioned my short grandmother in a pair of over-sized trousers standing before a circus mirror, making her resemble a munchkin. By the time we stopped laughing, we needed tissues to wipe our soppy eyes. Grandma struggled with a weight problem, but she knew how to dress for her figure and also when to laugh at herself.

I was fifteen when my grandparents sold their Savanna Street home and moved into a mobile home park in South Lawrence. I often pedaled my bike there on Sundays for a visit, sometimes arriving in time to catch the tail end of a Billy Graham sermon.

Grandma awoke early, baked a delicious coffee cake, and just before I arrived, started a kettle of water on the stove. Two China teacups sat side by side on a dainty white doily in the center of her kitchen table. Each teacup held our favorite teas, their tags dangled over the sides. Once inside, the sweet aroma of something baked readied my heart for a warm visit. With her short, broad arms and wide smile, she gave me an affectionate embrace that nearly swallowed me whole.

"Pick one," Grandma would say, referring to the two choices of tea.

Grandma and I became kindred spirits, I'd like to think because of our similar personalities and the faith we had in common, but also because we shared the same woman who inflicted pain and grieved our hearts. Our mutual suffering knitted our souls together.

With our teacups and coffee cake, we settled into her cozy living room. She played a record, left over from her years of owning a stereo and electronics business with her son, Robert. Grandma enjoyed good music. She also liked her music played loud. But not so loud we couldn't hear each other talk. The first time she played a record, she gave me a wide grin. My heart smiled. I knew I had no ordinary grandmother. Few grandmothers in the 70's owned and ran an electronics and records business. Even though we were two generations apart, we connected in this remarkable and memorable way. To me, Grandma was trendy and hip. It's no wonder the college students frequented the store.

Of course, the popular tunes of Fleetwood Mac, Kansas, Earth, Wind & Fire, the Rolling Stones, and other classics usually goaded Grandpa to grab his cowboy hat and keys and shuffle out the door. I don't know where Grandpa took off to, but I suspect he joined his buddies at the soda fountain where I worked.

Grandma and I could talk for hours, forgetting about time. She asked about school, my friends, my job, church, faith, my brother Mike and his budding Army career, and Davey and Timothy. And Grandma never missed an opportunity to share how the Lord had answered a prayer or how God stretched her financial resources to meet her needs. Sometimes I was a recipient of those blessed resources. And without fail, she remembered to ask about my dad.

Sometimes our visits were somber because of some ugly altercation with Mama. Sitting at the kitchen table, softer music of the Carpenters, Cat Stevens, Peter, Paul, and Mary, and Simon & Garfunkel played in the background, reminding me that we both had a little "old soul" in us. We cradled our cups of tea while the music soothed our concerned and hurting hearts. Our conversations were contemplative and reflective, yet sympathetic of the struggle Mama was in. Grandma was the spiritual matriarch in our family, but even she sometimes had nothing but uncertainties and desperate prayers in her heart.

During one visit, I asked Grandma what Mama was like as a little girl.

"She was smart for her age," Grandma answered pensively, "but she didn't like being held. She wasn't the type of child who welcomed being picked up and plopped onto someone's lap. She fussed and squirmed."

Knowing Grandpa was also fussy, irritable, and had a temper problem, I assumed Mama took after her father in this regard. But Grandma shared a startling confession. She said she also had an anger problem when she was much younger, but the Lord helped her overcome it. Learning this, I wondered how much of Mama and her brother Robert's childhood was actually happy in a home with two short-tempered parents.

Despite our close relationship, there was a lot I didn't share with Grandma for fear of Mama retaliating against her. I also sensed there was more hostile history between Mama and Grandma than she wanted to burden me with. My assumption was correct. In her journal, Grandma noted as much.

I pray for Lisa. I know her mother takes it out on her and browbeats her into submission over any crossing of her will.

March 7, 1980

Once, Grandma gingerly recommended to Mama that she see a mental health specialist. She even offered to pay for the two of them to go together, but Mama turned indignant and resentful at the suggestion. Her refusal grieved Grandma. She felt at a complete loss for how to help her daughter.

"You're the one who's sick and needs professional help!" Mama screamed one day when Grandma brought the subject up again. Angst, regret, and sorrow gnawed at my grandmother's soul. In her journal, she admitted she had made mistakes as a wife and mother, but her contrite heart communicated she asked for forgiveness and prayed for healing, both for Mama and their relationship.

We were going to have a good visit today, my daughter and I, but instead, it turned out awful. She began her usual accusation-that I'm not a good mother and never was to her-how Robert was my whole life that she needed emotional help because of my failures, and I didn't get it for her. She told me she hated me. Of course, these things hurt, but most of all I'm worried about her. She needs counseling and I need it to know how to cope with her ... I'm so worried that she is going to have a breakdown, and she's got those two precious little boys who need her. I'm emotionally drained. I can still hear her voice filled with anger and hatred screaming at me— "I'm sick of you—all of you—you're all so pious!" I had asked her to forgive me, but she refused. Her whole appearance changed before me. Her face contorted and eyes flashing as she utterly condemned everything I am. I have never seen demon possession, but the thought came to me that she acted and looked like it. I suggested counseling, but she said that I was the one who needed to go, then repeated her tirade against me with such loathing I'd never heard from anyone before. I tried to stay calm and reason with her, but this enraged her the most. She held my sins up to me and showed me times I had failed. I told her I had confessed my shortcomings, sins, and failures, yet she still called me a liar. I can't understand all of this. She has sinned and she cannot admit it even to herself. She feels forced to justify her sins by blaming the person who possesses the least threat to her. I prayed for her today to heal her. I love my daughter, my only daughter—she is as lost to me as if she were dead. I ask Jesus to help me.

March 6, 1980

Whatever sins Grandma allegedly committed, Mama wanted nothing to do with forgiveness. I couldn't fathom my grandmother doing something so awful that it was unforgivable. But by the same token, Grandma confronted Mama about her sharp tongue. In her journal, I discovered an entry of just how sharp Mama's tongue could be. Mama called me "that little bitch" during one of their arguments. It sickened Grandma, and she told Mama she'd regret those words. Mama resented such confrontation and refused to acknowledge the sin of calling her own daughter such an ugly term. Grandma kept the nastiest of Mama's ugliness private, penning her worst fears and torment in her journal, weaving them into prayers.

It troubled me that Mama possessed a spirit of discord and revenge—that she wanted her own mother and even me to suffer, but suffer for what? That was the ongoing mystery. There was something else, something I still pondered on, but I never spoke of it because even to me it seemed outlandish. Imagine my surprise when I read that Grandma had seen it too—in Mama's face, but neither one of us brought it up to the other. We both had wondered if a bad spirit, something like a demon had attached itself to Mama's personality or identity. Was that even possible? Mama's changing appearance, repugnant tongue and piercing dark eyes had scorched her soul, too. It was all too overwhelming. I didn't understand what was happening to Mama or why I was just as much the enemy as her own mother.

One day, before I left home, I heard Mama and Kevin arguing again about how his side of the family had excluded her from family gatherings. Mama was still troubled by that. Kevin reacted in his usual way when Mama became irate. He gave her the silent treatment and sometimes prefaced it with a warning.

"If you can't discuss our disagreements rationally, I refuse to talk to you," Kevin declared. At this, Mama became livid. She couldn't tolerate being spoken to like that. Enraged, she retaliated by spewing despicable words at him. I was horrified. My stepfather kept his composure, but his passive behavior sent Mama over the top. She called me into the argument and demanded I concur with her accusations against my stepfather. Caught in the middle, I was petrified. Thankfully, before I had to answer, he immediately interjected.

"So now you're going to enlist your own daughter in our disagreements?" Kevin asked sharply. Relieved, I quickly departed the room. Moments later, Mama ordered Kevin out of the house.

"And don't come back until you're ready to apologize!" Mama screamed at him as the kitchen door slammed behind him. Three days later, he arrived back. After apologizing, Mama allowed him back into the home.

I liked my stepfather, but that day I realized why Kevin had never intervened on my behalf. Like everyone else, his passive nature was no match for her domineering spirit. He was a victim of abuse, too.

In later years, I understood our home fulfilled the biblical verse of Mark 3:25, "And if a house is divided against itself, that house cannot stand." It also explained why my parents' home in California imploded.

Mama's acid-like anger, narcissistic control, and unforgiveness were incompatible with Kevin's passive, gentle demeanor, allowing

Satan to plant a spirit of division. The apostle Paul wrote, "If you forgive anyone anything, I too forgive ... for your sake in the presence of Christ to keep Satan from taking advantage of us; for we are not ignorant of his schemes" (2 Corinthians 2:10-11).

Paul warned us that if we withhold forgiveness, we are a pawn for Satan's evil strategies. Not only that, but when we refuse to renew our minds with His Word, we meet the biblical definition of "ignorant." This type of ignorance will put us at a disadvantage against our enemy. Satan took advantage of their opposing natures. We're on dangerous ground with a rebellious spirit and an unforgiving heart. Family strife that causes discord attracts Satan to gain a foothold in our thoughts, followed by a stronghold on our hearts. He takes particular delight in dysfunctional or broken families, recognizing a ripe environment for planting a seed for a generational curse. If you're a Proverbs 31 woman, you're called to stand in the gap and cover your home in prayer; otherwise, Proverbs 14:1b could be a consequence: "... but the foolish one [who lacks spiritual insight] tears it down with her own hands."

After leaving home, I carried the fear of failure into my future, and it influenced my early academic and vocational decisions. Mama constantly scrutinized my performance around the home. And her sharp criticisms led to a fear of taking reasonable risks. I became heavily preoccupied with not measuring up and I let opportunities go by. I did not live in the reality of 2 Timothy 1:7b, "... but He has given us a spirit of power and of love and of sound judgment ..." My emotions were battered, my self-confidence was low, and I had identity issues. I was a Christian, but a defeated Christian.

> The apostle Paul warned us that if we withhold forgiveness, we are a pawn for Satan's evil strategies.

In my quest to understand an unhealthy fear, I read that a spirit of fear is symbolized by the lizard. A fearful creature, it jumps at everything (Hickey, *Satan Proof Your Home* 73, 65). Daily, I walked on eggshells; my focus was simply not to provoke Mama. I remained like the lizard around her for years. Her calloused words, "You don't think. You don't use your head," or "You won't amount to anything," ruminated in my thoughts.

Of course, not every day was tumultuous. We did have good days. She *could* be congenial, and pleasant, but I was wary. Was this rational side really her, or was it part of her mental illness with fluctuating emotions and unpredictable behavior? With her need to manipulate and control, I couldn't trust any of it. However, whenever Mama was in a pleasant mood, it delighted Grandma. She recorded such moments.

Last night we drove to the farm for Davey's birthday. My daughter was so warm and loving that I just loved the whole evening. How I wish she and I could always get along so well.

June 30, 1980

But I never allowed such pleasant occasions to cause me to let my guard down. Today, I see things more discerningly. Grandma and Mama were in different spiritual realms—one shadowed in darkness and the other one in light. One's mental state so mystifying and nefarious, and the other, desperate to pull her daughter out of a dark abyss. Back then, watching their relationship crumble, I wondered, is this my own future with Mama? This worry added to my own suffering. For three generations of mothers and daughters, none of our souls were well. We each were fighting our own demons.

School offered me amnesty, but my stress amassed once again when the school bell rang at the end of the day. As the school bus got closer to my home, the knots in my stomach intensified until cramping and sharp jabs had me crouching in my seat. I dreaded coming home. Even when there was no indication something was wrong when I left each morning, I returned to the house in fear. Walking the long gravel driveway, the same questions plagued my anxious heart: What mood was Mama in? Were Mama and Kevin arguing? Had Mama and Grandma been fighting? And was I already in trouble? I retreated to my bedroom to do homework, hoping to stay off her radar until dinner. I was like the proverbial frog in the kettle of lukewarm water, unable to perceive the dangers lurking as troubling circumstances heated up. And here I was, unknowingly mired in a spirit of rejection, with dark forces encircling my own life. But the question was, "When the water boiled, who was going to pull me out of the kettle?"

* * * * * *

It was Sunday, July 6, two days after my awful altercation with Mama. Dad and I arrived at my grandparents' home. Stepping inside, Grandma and I embraced, holding each other a little bit tighter this time, confirming my suspicion that Grandma already knew about the falling out Mama and me had over the fruit trees. Grandpa, in his usual reserved manner, smiled and pulled me close for a side hug. Then Dad and Grandpa shook hands. Grandma's calm composure and warm hospitality comforted my disturbed spirit. Here, I felt safe and shored up with support.

I was confident that between the three of them, I'd receive wise counsel about how to move forward with Mama. But that wasn't exactly what took place.

"I called your mother this morning," Grandma said. "Your mother seemed to think I had already known about your quarrel with her. I hadn't, but of course she started to tell me everything. She was still angry, but towards the end of our conversation, she sounded as if she wanted to make things right. I sensed she felt awful about how you two ended it the other day."

I was shocked that Mama wanted to work this out so soon— it wasn't like her to do an about-face. But the thought of returning to the farm set my nerves into overdrive. My heart thumped faster. *I can't go back there. I can't do this,* I thought.

I don't know how, but I agreed to meet with Mama. It seemed too soon, but I did want to work things out. If for no other reason, I hoped it would make this awful pit in my stomach go away.

After our visit, Dad drove me back to my room at the Campus Christian House. As usual, we sat in the car for a few minutes, summarizing our time together. I always hated these emotional goodbyes—they were tough when I was a little girl, and now, at almost nineteen, they were no easier given my new circumstances. What I really wanted was reinforcements for my visit with Mama. I felt like David going up against Goliath, but without David's courage, just hanging on the hem of a prayer. Yet, I knew I had to go alone. If I brought anyone with me, Mama would see it as a sign of weakness—that I couldn't stand on my own.

Dad and I hugged and said our goodbyes. I waved until his car disappeared, my stomach still churning.

Studies show that emotional trauma creates wounds in areas of normal development of young people. If someone had done a scan on my brain the night I returned to the farm, I'd wager they would have found the area known as the amygdala blown up in red, sounding alarms. It's associated with the area of the brain that processes fear and emotion. It's also known that when the brain creates memories in a certain mood or emotional state, such as a traumatic experience like child abuse, those memories can go underground or become hidden in the brain and are not consciously accessed ("How Traumatic Memories").

I can relate to this medical finding because I only recall two things from the night I returned to the farm to see Mama: praying and driving there. I have no memory of meeting Mama or what we discussed.

Because of Grandma's journal entry, I knew the meeting took place, but also because I came away with a physical token, confirming our meeting was civil. It gave me hope.

Lisa and her mother patched things up—somewhat. Her mother gave her the pink sapphire ring that I gave to her several years ago. She will be angry at me for trying to help Lisa, plus her giving away the gift that I had given to her hurt just a little, but of course, if she didn't want it—then it's fine to pass it on to Lisa. Will all this never end? Lord, watch over Lisa and protect her from evil. Amen

July 6, 1980

CHAPTER EIGHT

The Mystery of the Sin of Iniquity

Unhealed issues don't disappear with time.
They are pushed into your children, health, etc.

—The Mind Journal

I have always been intrigued by the ruins of ancient cities. A trip to Egypt as a teenager touring the Valley of the Kings and the Great Pyramids of Giza piqued my interest in archeology. Learning about ancient civilizations gives us a look at the lives of the inhabitants, but ruins don't always offer answers to what ended their existence, whether it was the result of a natural disaster, a deadly pandemic, war, or the disappearance of a natural resource, like water. Interestingly, some civilizations may have ended because of the sin of iniquity. But what is iniquity, and how does it manifest various types of ruins in our own lives?

Isaiah 53:5a says, "He (Jesus) was wounded for our transgressions, he was bruised for our iniquities …" The word iniquity means to bend or to distort (the heart). It also implies a certain weakness or predisposition toward a certain sin. There's a difference between a sin committed, then repented and never done again, and iniquity, which is a sin practiced as part of one's lifestyle. Given certain circumstances or the "right" environment, a person will "bend" in that direction (Hickey, *Breaking Generational Curses* 21).

You Shall Have No Other Gods Before Me

In chapter four, we learned about the practice of gradually moving boundary stones to expand property, a transgression that can lead to a lifestyle of sin. The Ten Commandments also represent boundary stones. Not merely suggestions, but commands, and not for past generations, but for all generations. Notice God's first commandment: "I am the LORD your God, who has brought you out of the land of Egypt, out of the house of slavery. You shall have no other gods before Me" (Exodus 20:2-3).

Have you ever considered why God listed this commandment first? In His wisdom, He knew that anything we place above Him leads to bondage. God freed the Israelites from Egypt, but their continued freedom depended on obeying this commandment because idolatry inevitably leads back to captivity.

When we think of idol worship, we often recall the golden calf, but the calf symbolizes today's idols. Though God blesses us with much, our sin nature makes resisting modern idols a constant struggle. Misplaced priorities, dissatisfaction, hardships, and insecurities can lure us into idol worship, pushing God aside. Ultimately, any idol we chase leads to the same result: bondage, which traps us in more sin and further separates us from God.

> When we think of idol worship, we often recall the golden calf, but the calf symbolizes today's idols as well.

God takes idolatry seriously, but in His love and grace, He always provides a way out. In Exodus 34:16 He instructed the Israelites not to intermarry with certain groups who worshiped other gods. This command was crucial, as explained in Deuteronomy 7:3-4. "You shall not intermarry with them; you shall not give your daughter to his son, nor shall you take his daughter for your son; for they will turn your sons away from following Me to serve other gods ..."

God warned the Israelites not to intermarry with those who worshiped other gods to prevent apostasy—abandoning their faith in Him and embracing false gods.

The wisdom in Deuteronomy 7:3-4 applies today. Marrying an unbeliever can lead us into the same trap, tempting our hearts to turn from God and worship modern idols like materialism, money, technology, power, prestige, self, and pleasure.

But iniquity includes more than idolatry; it encompasses behaviors and weaknesses that pass through generations, such as abandonment, broken family structures, substance abuse, anger, depression, mental illness, adultery, abuse, and rejection. Allowing these iniquities unchecked access to our lives compromises our walk with God and becomes a stumbling block for future generations.

Visiting the Iniquity of the Fathers

Earlier we read in Exodus 20:3, "... You shall have no other gods before Me." Just two verses later there is an interesting phrase, "... visiting the iniquity of the fathers ..." (Exodus 20:5). Let's look at the word, "visiting."

It's easy to discuss the iniquities that have harmed our families, like parental rejection. We may seek advice or confirmation from trusted people about the hurtful behavior of a parent. While it's important to support one another as Christians, Beth Moore, in her Bible study *Breaking Free*, offers an important perspective. She says:

God never called us to preserve our ancient ruins. Rather than inspect the ancient ruins and then work with God to rebuild, we just keep revisiting and preserving and we never get over it. (87)

If we only talk, blame, and complain about family inequities we're just visiting and preserving those ruins. Like archaeologists excavating physical ruins, we can examine generational iniquities to understand their impact. By exploring the lives of our parents, grandparents, and beyond, we can certainly identify and address these entrenched issues in our own generation, but we do so with the intention of preventing them from becoming a stumbling block in our generation and the next.

The Mystery of Iniquities

Unrepented iniquities lead to bondage. As we examine past generations' ruins, we must also check if we've imposed bondage on ourselves and if we've planted iniquities in the next generation's hearts. The Bible calls this the "mystery of iniquity," which author Marilyn Hickey defines as the hidden link between a parent's sins and their children's paths (Hickey, *Breaking Generational Curses* 23).

> The definition of "the mystery of iniquity," is that hidden link between a parent's sins, and their children's paths. -Marilyn Hickey, *Breaking Generational Curses*

The Power and Consequences of Iniquity

After settling in the Promised Land, the Israelites continued disobeying God, believing they could succeed without His help. They became stubborn and backslidden, choosing to worship the surrounding nations' gods. Regrettably, "the Israelites did evil in the sight of the Lord, and they forgot the Lord their God …" (Judges 3:7). But God didn't give up on His wayward children. In the book of Judges, He raised up certain men and women, known as judges, to lead God's people back into a relationship with Him, offering a way out of a life of sin. Joshua, who took Moses' place of leading the

Israelites into the Promised Land, was a judge. After he died and the generation that was with Joshua also died, "another generation rose after them who did not know (recognize, understand) the LORD, nor even the work which He had done for Israel" (Judges 2:10). This generation, though freed from Egypt, failed to pass on a spiritual legacy to the next, as noted in Deuteronomy 6:7.

You shall teach them diligently to your children [impressing God's precepts on their minds and penetrating their hearts with His truths] and shall speak of them when you sit in your house and when you walk on the road and when you lie down and when you get up.

Instead of teaching their children about God, they paved a well-trampled path of disobedience and idolatry. This new generation, after Joshua's generation, continued in idolatry. Despite God's repeated efforts to turn their hearts back to Him, their iniquity was deeply entrenched. This defiance angered God, leading to consequences in which He withdrew His support, causing their enemies to defeat them in battle. Notice, God withdrew His support, not His love.

When the LORD raised up judges for them, He was with the judge and He rescued them from the hand of their enemies all the days of the judge ... But when the judge died, they turned back and behaved more corruptly than their fathers, in following and serving other gods and bowing down to them ... So the anger of the LORD burned against Israel, and He said, Because this nation has transgressed My covenant, which I commanded their fathers, and has not listened to My voice, I also will no longer drive out before them any of the nations which Joshua left [to be conquered] when he died ... so the LORD allowed those nations to remain. (Judges 2:18–21, 23)

Rather than destroying the Israelites, God chose to discipline them out of compassion and mercy. He allowed pagan nations to remain because He intended for the Israelites to be a light to other nations. However, they rejected His plan, continued in sin, and violated God's command by intermarrying with pagan nations. Until they repented and abandoned idolatry, God allowed them to be conquered by these wicked nations.

In Judges 3:8, the word "sold" indicates God's ownership of His people, as only an owner can sell what belongs to him. Here, it refers to God delivering the Israelites into the hands of their enemy, the King of Mesopotamia, and into bondage once more. After eight years,

> ... the Israelites cried out to the LORD [for help], the LORD raised up a man (another way out) to rescue the people of Israel, Othniel, the son of Kenaz, Caleb's younger brother. He (Othniel) went out to war, and the LORD gave the king of Mesopotamia into his (Othniel's) hand. (Judges 3:9–10)

Othniel defeated the king of Mesopotamia. But once Othniel died, the Israelites went back to their wicked ways, and the LORD gave Israel into the hands of Eglong, king of Moab (Judges 3:11-13). During the eighteenth year of captivity to the king of Moab, "the Israelites cried out to the LORD [for help]; the LORD raised up a man to rescue them, Ehud the son of Gera, a Benjamite ..." (Judges 3:15).

The cycle of sin, bondage, repentance, and freedom left the Israelites both physically captive and spiritually bankrupt. Like ancient landowners who moved boundary stones to expand their property, the Israelites adjusted the first commandment by worshiping false gods. Similarly, if we alter God's commandments to fit our lifestyles, we risk facing negative consequences.

God's people remained off track, but in His mercy, He sent prophets like Isaiah to warn them of impending judgment if they didn't abandon their idols. Ignoring the warnings, they faced destruction when King Nebuchadnezzar II of Babylon attacked Jerusalem in 586 BC. The city and temple were destroyed, and the people were exiled to Babylon for seventy years. Despite this, Isaiah 61:1-2 contains a prophetic promise of hope for their eventual release and better times.

The Spirit of the Lord God is upon me because the LORD has anointed and commissioned me (Isaiah) to bring good news to the humble and afflicted; He has sent me to bind up [the wounds of] the brokenhearted, To proclaim release [from confinement and condemnation] to the [physical and spiritual] captives And freedom to prisoners … to comfort all who mourn …

The promise manifested through King Cyrus of Persia when he overthrew the Babylonians and allowed the exiled Jews to return to Jerusalem. They began rebuilding the city, the temple, and the wall, as well as their lives. Although they faced significant challenges, God provided them with a new blueprint for restoration and rebuilding. He promised "the oil of joy instead of mourning, the garment [expressive] of praise instead of a disheartened spirit" (Isaiah 61:3). And He promised that "they would be called the trees of righteousness [strong and magnificent, distinguished for integrity, justice, and right standing with God]" (v. 3). God promised them double blessings and renewed joy (Isaiah 61:7). Isaiah 61 also offers us a promise of hope through Jesus, who came to heal those bound by generational ruins, sin, and despair. He promises to turn our mourning into joy as well.

My friend, if you're still bound in captivity and living amongst your generational ruins and your life needs rebuilding, claim Isaiah 61 for your circumstances. Write it down on an index card and put it in a place where it will always be before you. If you cry out to Him, He'll answer. He responds to a heart turned to Him. Even if your life resembles the lives of those ancient Israelites, wandering in and out of spiritual bondage, God has a new blueprint for your life that includes building a new foundation. All He requires is that you call out to Him.

He Has Sent Me

The Hebrew word to "bind up" in Isaiah 61:1 is *chavash*, which means to bind, bind up, or bind on and to wrap. The Hebrew word for a "broken heart" is *lev shavur*, meaning to "break or tear into pieces" (Moore 97–98). To appreciate the deeper meaning, read Hosea 6:1: "Come and let us return [in repentance] to the LORD, For He has torn us, but He will heal us; He has wounded us, but He will bandage us."

The book of Hosea also addresses the unfaithfulness of the Israelites towards God, but it reveals an interesting comparison. The ungodly behavior of the Israelites parallels the personal life of the prophet Hosea's wife. It's a beautiful story of a man's love for his wife who was caught up in a sinful lifestyle and his desire to draw her back to himself. Hosea's wife, Gomer, left Hosea on several occasions to return to a life of a prostitute. The book of Hosea compares Israel's unfaithfulness to that of a harlot. Like Hosea, who bought (redeemed) his wife back and continued to love her, God did the same with the unfaithful Israelites. Hosea's love for his wife symbolizes God's love for His people. Their own sin broke their hearts (*lev shavur*), but out of obedience, they repented, and God bound up their wounds (*chavash*) as if He literally gathered them up and wrapped a bandage around their hearts. Hosea's story is a literal reminder of God's heart towards us. Whether we've faced withheld blessings or rejection, Jesus offers comfort, grace, and love to heal our crushed spirits. He can transform our ruins into something new and meaningful if we allow Him access to our hurts.

By examining the lives of God's people, we see how generational sin begets bondage. Each generation adds to the overall iniquity, further weakening the resistance of the next generation to sin. If the family tree is not cleansed of iniquity, then each generation becomes worse and will do what their parents, grandparents, and great-grandparents did (Hickey, *Breaking Generational Curses* 21–22).

Even though Jesus has already borne our sins, iniquities, and transgressions, a Christian can still be in bondage if he or she continues to exercise the iniquity. This means the iniquity hasn't been broken in that generation. Marilyn Hickey's definition of an unbroken iniquity is: "An uncleansed iniquity that increases in strength from one generation to the next, affecting the members of that family and all who come into relationship with that family" (Hickey, *Breaking Generational Curses* Chart 2).

Deliverance from Iniquity's Curse

God's promise in Isaiah 61:4 was fulfilled with the temple and city wall's reconstruction, but the chapter's main focus is the restoration of hearts, homes, and lives. It's a blessing that God ensures nothing is left out in the restoration process. "Then they will rebuild the ancient ruins; they will raise up and restore the former desolations; and they will renew the ruined cities, the desolations of many generations" (Isaiah 61:4).

Did you notice how many times Isaiah used the word "will?" What God wills cannot be undone. Some of the generational ruins in my mother's family lineage are anger, bitterness, abandonment, rejection, untreated mental illness, and abuse. I include mental illness because Mama refused to be treated, refused to own her ungodly actions, and allowed it to manifest into sin. These were the "former desolations" in my mother's, grandparents', and great-grandparents' generation, but not in mine. I still made mistakes as a parent, but I refused to be bound in anger and bitterness. By giving God access to those former desolations in my heritage, He helped me build a new foundation. It wasn't a one-and-done fix. It took time, years really, because as my children grew, the former desolations of Mama's generation would encroach back into my life as she continued to dispense unloving offenses. But I kept returning to the Lord for mending of my wounded emotions. And as I did, God dispensed His truth, and I moved forward in His grace.

Don't let fear, others' opinions, or the belief that it's too late keep you from seeking healing. It's not God's will for you to live under rejection or bondage. If a parent has stepped back, Jesus is ready to stand in the gap for you. When in my darkest pit of pain, I trusted in Psalm 27:10. "Although my father and my mother have abandoned me, Yet the LORD will take me up [adopt me as His child]." Wait for and expect the Lord to bring you out of the "horrible pit ... and set your feet upon a rock ... and a new song in your mouth and a praise to God" (Psalm 40:2-3).

Of course, the devil will do whatever he can to stall or stop your progress to keep you in bondage. Three men named Sanballat, Tobiah, and Geshem opposed Nehemiah's wall reconstruction (Nehemiah 2:19; 4:1-3) when the Israelites returned home after their release from exile. Nehemiah led his people in prayer and vigilance, encouraging them not to be discouraged, despite opposition. Similarly, you may face obstacles to healing but pray for discernment. God promises in Romans 8:28 to bring good from all circumstances, but if we give up or resist His healing, the springs of life become dammed up and cannot flow freely to the next generation.

It Only Takes One

Despite the dark implication of the mystery of iniquity, we can have freedom. But we have to be willing to excavate the ruins, understand their origins, and explore whether your family line has lingering sins of iniquity that need to be repented of and cut off. The good news is that, because of Jesus, we are no longer held responsible for the iniquities of our forefathers; however, we are still held accountable for our own. Each generation has the chance to break the cycle of iniquity, and it just takes one person to change the trajectory of a family line. By ending a particular iniquity, a new generation can live in the freedom God intended.

Just as God appointed Nehemiah to rebuild the wall around Jerusalem, you are called to be the foreman of a new construction project for your generation. God equips us to be overcomers. This journey won't be fast or easy, but it will be worth it. If needed, seek a godly counselor who understands rejection to help address destructive patterns, develop boundaries, and regain control of your spiritual and emotional health. We have a fierce God. The notion that we can't change is a lie the devil wants us to believe. Don't remain blinded by his lies. God's Word says in Jeremiah 33:3: "Call to Me and I will answer you and tell you [and even show you] great and mighty things, [things which have been confined and hidden], which you do not know and understand and cannot distinguish." As you read, you'll see how God revealed truth, truth about myself, the dark dynamics of my relationship with my mother, and God's nature.

It's time to walk in truth. You'll have an authentic journey with the Lord and if you're a parent, you'll be a godly influence on your children, whether they are grown or not, leaving a spiritual legacy for generations that follow.

CHAPTER NINE

MAMA'S REVELATION

Perception of ourself is a powerful force;
it can lead us to or away from our purpose in life.

—Lisa N. Phillips

Sitting on the porch swing one evening at the women's Campus Christian House, I was troubled by thoughts of my cat, Jody. I felt betrayed having to find Jody a new home. It hurt that Mama had been so cruel. Thankfully, a former high school friend offered to take Jody in, but my friend couldn't be sure he'd stick around. I cried knowing that I'd likely never see my beloved cat again. Grandma had written in her journal that Mama and I tentatively patched things up, but my heart needed more than a patch.

It was dusk when I stood up to go inside. That's when I saw the door of the men's Campus Christian House open and a young man step out. Closing the door behind him, he looked in my direction, then skipped down the porch steps and headed towards me.

"You must be new here," he hollered, as he crossed the two joined lawns. "Hi, I'm Cory."

"Yeah, I moved in a week ago. I'm Lisa. Nice to meet you." I closed the door to face him. Emotionally, I was drained and wasn't in a talking mood, but to send him away felt rude. I sat back down on the porch swing.

"During the school year these two houses are full," Cory explained, "but during the summer, they empty out."

"I figured, which worked out good for me," I replied. "So, why are you still here?"

He chuckled at my question then took a seat in the chair opposite me. He had a lean build, and I figured him to be at least six feet tall. Now in the glow of the porch light, I could better see his facial features. He had a good head of dark, straight hair, cut short around his ears and parted down one side, then swooped to the other side. I had never seen such deep-set eyes; they gave his whole countenance a melancholy look, yet his voice and demeanor didn't come across that way.

"Last summer I did go back home, but this summer I decided to stay in Lawrence," he answered.

"Where's home?"

"Overland Park. My mom is an English teacher, and my dad runs a business in the downtown business district. So, what brings you to the Campus Christian House?"

"I'm originally from Lawrence. But I moved from McAllister. Then a week ago my mother and I had a falling out—thankfully, I ended up here."

"I'm sorry to hear that, but I think you'll like being a part of the Campus Christian organization."

That evening, I learned Cory was in the music program at the University of Kansas. Piano and competitions had been a large part of his life growing up.

As the evening progressed, I found myself enjoying his company. We shared snippets about our lives and families; his parents had been married thirty-five years, and his sister, Debbie, was a soprano singer in her own right. Cory spoke well of his childhood, and likewise of his parents; they both had been encouraging and emotionally supportive. Cory's traditional values shaped his spiritual development, and he felt honor-bound to uphold them. He was grateful to his parents and, like many young men, wanted to make his dad proud.

Cory had interests beyond music, including business, government, and politics. As we discussed our college pursuits, his dreams, though varied, revealed a high level of confidence and intense motivation. He was ambitious, but humble, aware that some goals would require hard work, which he was willing to undertake.

By comparison, I struggled with other people's opinions, and this affected my self-confidence. Except for a dream to be a schoolteacher, the only other vocation I considered was to follow in my dad's footsteps into the airline industry as a flight attendant. From my airplane seat, I would study their poise and professionalism. But I was short. At five feet tall with a petite 105-pound frame, I felt I was the wrong stature. And maybe I was, but I also had the wrong mindset. I had allowed what I *wasn't* to negatively affect my self-esteem. Perception of one's self is a powerful force; it can lead us to or away from our purpose in life. I did not have that "professional woman" look of a flight attendant. I compared myself to what I saw advertised in the 1970's during the women's liberation movement. I wasn't tall and lean and couldn't visualize myself wearing a tailored suit with high heels and carrying a briefcase. Most women in the 60's and 70's worked as secretaries, clerical workers, teachers, nurses, and bookkeepers. Songs such as "I am Woman," by Helen Reddy, released in 1972, empowered women to break the glass ceiling. I sang that song myself, later as a teenager. But for me, it had the opposite effect. To see these professional women portrayed in the media reinforced a subconscious message that I had to *look* like that in order to *be* like that. Unfortunately, I held that image in my head as the only standard for success. I carried a flawed perception of my potential; it would eventually lead me to make a vocational mistake I would later regret.

Just before the evening ended, we landed on a subject we had in common: reading. Cory enjoyed the literary works of all the classics including Ernest Hemingway, John Updike, John Steinbeck, even Shakespeare, and others. It was obvious he clearly had a literary advantage having a mother as a high school English teacher.

"Since you like piano, would you be interested in joining me on campus while I put in some practice time?" my neighbor asked.

His invite caught me by surprise. Did he just ask me out? By the time our porch talk ended, we made plans to get together the following Sunday.

* * * * * *

Murphy Hall on the college campus was nothing I had expected, but neither was Cory's musical talent. Inside the building were long hallways with small practice rooms one after another for the music students. As we searched for a vacant room, a cacophony of sounds filled the hallway. Finally finding one, we stepped inside. In the center sat a single piano.

"Wow, it feels …"

"Institutional?" Cory finished my sentence.

"Yeah, exactly, like a room in a psych ward, but without the padded walls. How many hours a week do you spend in one of these rooms?"

"During the school year—a lot," he said.

Cory took his seat on the piano bench and positioned his long legs to comfortably rest on the foot pedals. I stood slightly off to his right. He began with a warm-up. He ran his long, slender fingers down the length of the keyboard in a rapid fashion then reversed the direction. It was captivating. He did this a few more times, and then he was ready.

He set his sheet music on the piano, took a deep breath, then slowly exhaled. While his upper body relaxed, mine was growing excited. Composed, he gently placed his hands on a section of keys. He lowered his head slightly, then closed his eyes for a moment as if to align his body to the music already streaming in his head. The room went silent. Then, he raised his right hand off the keyboard, his wrist hung limp while his left hand began to play the keys. Seconds later, his right hand came down slowly, gracefully; his fingers lightly kissing the keys. Delicate music flowed from the Steinway; it was beautiful … moving. He swayed his head slowly to the right and to the left, his eyes remained closed as the music consumed his whole body. Roughly a minute passed; the music suddenly became intense and loud, startling me. His fingers danced all over the keyboard, moving faster and faster, racing up and down the length of the keyboard. It was exhilarating and hypnotic. Then, the tempo suddenly changed again, returning to the measure and rhythm he began with, then another round of passionate hammering of the keys, lasting another minute, ending with gingerly pressing a set of keys with both hands, holding them down until the piano was quiet. He raised his head, took a deep breath, and slowly exhaled. Cory turned to look at me, his hair around his forehead damp.

"Wow! That was incredible. It was like a private concert—all from the guy living next door. You're good."

"Thanks, I've been working on that piece all summer."

I can't recall what classical number he played, nor who the original composer was. I was too enthralled by the experience. All I knew was that I had been thoroughly entertained and loved it.

Mid-August arrived, and once again I loaded up my belongings into my '68 Malibu and drove the short distance to the new Campus Christian House. More curious than desperate this time, I parked in the driveway and studied the large, white Federal-style home with its symmetrical windows and black shutters. It was move-in day. As students came and went, carrying their possessions, I wondered which room would be mine.

The co-ed living arrangement required clear boundaries. The girls had the third floor and the men, the second. The house also came with house parents. Mark and Samatha lived on the first floor in their own apartment, overseeing the house—scheduling students to cook the evening meals, kitchen clean-up, and routine chores. On Tuesdays, Mark ran the evening Bible studies.

I stepped inside the spacious entrance. Facing me was the grand staircase, the wide steps covered in carpet long past its prime. Living and dining rooms were on my left with vintage rugs over the weathered wood flooring. Students sat on the equally worn couch and chairs positioned in front of the fireplace, discussing their class schedules, degree programs, summer jobs, and room assignments. The long, formal dining room was enclosed by a glass partition framed in wood that ran parallel to the living room. In the middle was a set of glass French doors. A long antique table took up nearly the entire length of the dining room. Antiquated lead glass chandeliers hung from the ceiling, producing sparkly colors. Everything about the place was old, but it had a fairy tale feel to it. As I gazed about, the thought of living in such a place seemed impossible, yet here I was.

"Welcome to the Campus Christian House," Samantha said, with a welcoming smile. "Are you checking in?"

"Yes." I gave her my name and she scanned her list, making a check mark by my name.

"The women's rooms are on the third floor. At the top of the stairs go to the right and your room is the last one on the left. You can start moving your things in."

I thanked her then headed to the staircase, taking in the familiar odor of an old house, reminding me of my paternal grandparents' home. Stopping at the first platform, between the first and second floors, I glanced up, taking in the height and breadth of the vertical space above me and the wood banister winding around each quarter turn. The house felt like a mansion.

A flutter of excitement rushed through me when I stepped inside my new room; it was the same room behind the largest dormer window I saw from inside my car. The sun was out strong and wide bands of brightness stretched across the floor. Tiny dust particles gleamed in the light as they floated about. Against the wall was a bunk bed. Scanning the room, I mentally placed my antique trunk under the dormer window. I thought of my parents, wishing one of them could have been here on such an important day.

Later, my roommate, Sue, arrived. Sue was from the small town of Eudora, east of Lawrence, and was also a freshman. While unpacking and organizing our room together we became better acquainted. She was easy to talk to and we hit it off immediately. Additional female students arrived, and laughter and chatty conversations spilled over into the hallway as they found their rooms and new roommates.

By early evening, the ambiance of the house became spirited and energetic, loud and excited voices bellowed from every floor, drawing me in. Now with even more enthusiasm, I looked forward to what was ahead.

Later that evening, Cory moved in. A student from Japan, named Osamu, became his roommate; the two would become good friends. On the third evening, Mark and Samantha, our house parents, prepared a meet-and-greet spaghetti meal. At 6:30 p.m. all my housemates filtered in. I stood at one end of the long dining room table along with thirty-two other students. The scene before me reminded me of the Last Supper. As I scanned my new housemates, I took a moment to reflect on where I was, how I got here, and how extraordinary it all seemed. Moments later, Mark led us in prayer. Like one big family, we passed around plates of fresh French bread, bowls of salad, and pasta as chatter commenced. To be surrounded by such welcoming and unassuming students was comforting and liberating. Just six months earlier, I had no idea I'd find myself here. I knew God made a way for me. He had done this. Grateful for such a place, it seemed surreal.

College was harder than expected, especially my English class. I had never studied Shakespeare in my small-town high school. Additionally, I dreaded Algebra as I did not have a math brain. The dining room of the Campus Christian House quickly became the hub for students burning the midnight oil doing homework, studying for exams, and writing papers. In order to understand Shakespeare or figure out how to solve for X, Cory, with his extensive literary knowledge and brain for numbers, helped me with my assignments. Despite my academic struggles, I never took college or my new home for granted. I loved my new life and settled right in.

Then one day in mid-October, while in my room studying, I heard a fellow male student call for me from the staircase landing. I rushed out of my room.

"There's a woman downstairs that wants to see you. She says she's your mother."

His words took me by surprise. Since I had moved out, Mama had never come to visit me. After our talk the night she gave me the sapphire ring, I had made a few trips to the farm, hoping it would keep the door of her heart open to me. Those visits, while they went without incident, were not without anxiety. Going there and seeing Mama was difficult, but I did what I thought was my duty, what a good daughter ought to do, or should do. But with each visit, I wondered, would she insult me with cruel digs, or point out all my faults and start a fight? Or would she criticize Grandma and shame me for having a relationship with her? Before Mama's nervous breakdown when I was nine, I had my basic needs met, and Mama had been caring and loving, though not overly affectionate. Didn't this mean I still should continue honoring her?

Sprinting down the staircase, I wondered why she had come. If she was in an angry state of mind, I worried she'd make a scene in front of my housemates. As I reached the last set of stairs, I saw Mama in the entryway, looking uncomfortable. We greeted each other, but there was no embrace.

"Can we go somewhere else?" she asked. Her disposition wasn't angry, and she didn't seem annoyed, but her candor made me uneasy. I was already assuming I had done something wrong, and she had come to browbeat me.

We stood beside my car in the driveway. We spoke about how my classes were going, but all I could think about was what kind of trouble I was in. Why else had she come? And then she got to the purpose of her impromptu visit. Her news hit me hard.

"I think you should know that your grandfather sexually abused me while I was growing up,"

I stood looking at Mama's face, flabbergasted and speechless, trying to process such a reprehensible act. I didn't see that one coming.

"You didn't know it, but I protected you around your grandfather when you were little," she added.

My mind raced back in time—to when we lived with my grandparents on Savanna Street right after we left Dad and California. Perhaps she was right because I had no memory of ever being alone with my grandfather.

It wasn't like Mama to wait for my response, but this time she did. Even though we had started talking again, I was reluctant to say too much for fear I'd trigger an emotional outburst in the driveway. I still got tongue-tied when talking to her. And everything I spoke had to be weighed against how she'd receive it and the likely consequences. I took the initiative and leaned towards her and gave her a hug. She didn't know quite what to do with my embrace; it seemed to catch her off guard.

"I'm sorry, Mama," I managed to say. "How long did this go on?"

"Many years."

I cringed inside, thinking for a moment about the implication of this, what it all meant, and how devastating her childhood must have been. Given her hostile background and wounding, I still couldn't trust her, but looking at her, she was visibly distressed, even vulnerable. But Mama wasn't finished. She had more to say.

Mama's tone became agitated. "Your grandmother said she didn't know what my father was doing, but I don't believe her."

My body tensed up. Things started to make sense. It explained the reason behind their hostile arguments. If Grandpa had abused her and Grandma knew, it also made sense why she had such bitterness towards her.

Right there, I decided to believe Mama's allegation. I couldn't verify the abuse and had no intention of confronting my grandparents, but I also wouldn't pass judgment on them. This is another aspect of why incest is so ugly; innocent relationships like mine and my grandmother's hung in the balance. I decided I'd stay impartial. At nineteen, I felt this new revelation was over my head, plus I didn't want to be in the middle of another dispute. Emotionally, I couldn't take on more conflict. In the background of my life, I was still processing my own trauma with Mama, and I needed space. Space to develop my own identity. Space to succeed in college, make new friends and have healthy relationships—and that included my relationship with my grandmother. But Mama's demeanor was undeniably different. And I wondered what prompted her to come and tell me. For whatever reason, she didn't demand anything from me as we wrapped up our visit. It seemed she just wanted me to know.

For the remainder of the day, I struggled to get back to my homework. My thoughts were tangled and disorganized. Mama's news disturbed me. I contemplated her childhood. Growing up in the 1940's and 50's, discussing incest was considered a cultural taboo. It wasn't a topic brought out into the light, even for counseling. And Mama's accusation that Grandma knew? I was perplexed about that. Later, after receiving Grandma's journal, I wondered if this is what Grandma had meant when she had asked for forgiveness for all the ways she had failed her daughter, but Mama refused it. I thought of my relationship with my grandmother. We had something sweet and special since I was a little girl. I couldn't let that go.

* * * * * *

Amidst our busy college schedules, Cory and I began dating but prioritized our education. Cory's encouragement helped me through my challenging first semester, and I found myself falling in love with his positive, adventurous, easygoing nature.

My first year at the Campus Christian House had been a blessing—new friends, more control over my life, spiritual growth, and dating a principled man. It had been a tough, bittersweet year, but with Mama's revelation, there was still much that wasn't well with my soul.

Stay tuned. The journey doesn't end here. Rejection had already carved deep scars into Lisa's life—but an even more brutal wounding lay in wait, exposing hard truths she didn't see coming. In Book Two, coming soon, the ominous darkness of an evil presence intensifies and the unrelenting soul-ache tightens after an unexpected loss. Yet, in the raw desperation of a broken life, a promise from the ancient pages of the Old Testament is whispered—just in the nick of time."

Works Cited

"Father's Impact on Child Development." *All for Kids*, 05/12/2023, https://www.all4kids.org/news/blog/a-fathers-impact-on-child-development, 6/7/2018.

"How Traumatic Memories Hide in the Brain, and How to Retrieve Them." *Science Daily*, August 17, 2015, www.sciencedaily.com/releases/2015/08/150817132325.htm.

"The Three Parts of Man–Spirit, Soul, and Body." *Blog: The Human Spirit*, www.biblesforamerica.org.

Bubeck, Ph.D. Mark, "Defeating Satan's Footholds and Strongholds." *Preach It Teach It*, November 7, 2016, https://preachitteachit.org/articles/defeating-satans-footholds-and-strongholds/.

Cachila, JB, "3 Ways Christians Give the Devil a Foothold in Their Lives." *The Christian Post*, June 5, 2017, https://www.christianpost.com/trends/3-ways-christians-give-the-devil-a-foothold-in-their-lives.html.

Chinn, Ed, "When Your Anger Gets the Best of You." *Focus on the Family*, February 1, 2007, www.focusonthefamily.com/get-help/when-your-anger-gets-the-best-of-you/.

Cloud, Ph.D. Henry and John Townsend, Ph.D. *Boundaries.* Zondervan, Grand Rapids, MI. 1992.

Cloud, Ph.D. Henry. *Changes that Heal.* Zondervan, Grand Rapids, MI. 1992.

Eckhardt, John. *Destroying the Spirit of Rejection*. Charisma House, Lake Mary, FL. 2016.

Foster, David Kyle, "Why Some People Remain in Sin, Bondage and Brokenness." *The Christian Post*, May 11, 2019, https://www.christianpost.com/voices/why-remain-in-sin-bondage-brokenness-david-kyle-foster.html.

Hickey, Marilyn, *Breaking Generational Curses*. Harrison House, Inc., Tulsa, OK. 2000.

Hickey, Marilyn. *Satan Proof Your Home*. Marilyn Hickey Ministries, Englewood, CO. 2018.

Johnson, Dale, "Destroying Strongholds." *Association of Certified Biblical Counselors*, October 5, 2020, https://biblicalcounseling.com/resource-library/podcast-episodes/destroying-strongholds/

Meyer, Joyce, "Be Transformed, Not Conformed," commentary in *Battlefield of the Mind Bible*, Faith Words, New York, NY. 2017.

Moore, Beth. *Breaking Free Workbook, Making Liberty in Christ a Reality in Life*, LifeWay Press, Nashville, TN. 1999.

Phillips, Lisa. *Faith Steps for Military Families*. Morgan James Publishing, Manhattan, NY. 2014.

pneuma. Merriam-Webster Dictionary. https://www.merriam-webster.com/dictionary/pneuma.

The Crossing Church, "Footholds & Strongholds," https://www.crossingparagould.com., November 7, 2016.

Trent, Ph.D. John and Gary Smalley, Ph.D. *The Blessing*. Thomas Nelson, Nashville, TN. 1993.

ABOUT THE AUTHOR

L isa Phillips, a retired military wife and mom is a certified children's coach, working with kids, ages 6-13.

Drawing on her former Pre-K teaching background, Lisa is an advocate for the mental wellness of kids and works one-on-one, in groups, and in workshops to develop strong mindset skills for success in school and in life. She uses a unique story-based approach, through the Adventures in Wisdom™ coaching program, developed by Renaye Thornborrow and endorsed by Jack Canfield.

As a WISDOM children's coach, she teaches children the tools needed to overcome issues such as bullying, peer pressure, low self-confidence, fears, major life challenges, integrity, respect, and others – offering tools and skills for emotional resilience before a crisis takes root.

She and her husband, Ray, have two grown children. When not writing, she enjoys time with family—especially her granddaughter, Rylee—and retreats to their 1910 log cabin on Cypress Island, Washington, where she savors a slower pace, meaningful conversations, and the quiet beauty of nature, God's grace, and beautiful blessings.

You can contact Lisa at:

https://www.AuthorLisaPhillips.net
https://www.CoachLisaPhillips.com

https://www.facebook.com/lisa.a.phillips.737
https://www.facebook.com/LisaPhillipsAuthor

https://www.instagram.com/CoachLisaPhillips

https://www.linkedin.com/in/AuthorLisaPhillips

www.ingramcontent.com/pod-product-compliance
Lightning Source LLC
Chambersburg PA
CBHW031428120626
46545CB00006B/2320